Getting Started with Magento Extension Development

Understand Magento extensions, and build your own from scratch!

Branko Ajzele

[PACKT] open source
PUBLISHING
community experience distilled

BIRMINGHAM - MUMBAI

Getting Started with Magento Extension Development

First published: September 2013

Production Reference: 1180913

Published by Packt Publishing Ltd.
Livery Place
35 Livery Street
Birmingham B3 2PB, UK

ISBN 978-1-78328-039-1

www.packtpub.com

Cover Image by Aniket Sawant (aniket_sawant_photography@hotmail.com)

Credits

Author
Branko Ajzele

Reviewers
Matej Krivak
Andrea De Pirro
Alistair Stead

Acquisition Editor
Akram Hussain

Commissioning Editor
Priyanka Shah

Technical Editors
Novina Kewalramani
Amit Ramadas
Rohit Kumar Singh

Project Coordinator
Romal Karani

Proofreader
Jonathan Todd

Indexer
Priya Subramani

Graphics
Ronak Dhruv

Production Coordinator
Conidon Miranda

Cover Work
Conidon Miranda

About the Author

Branko Ajzele is a professional, certified, and highly experienced software developer, focused on e-commerce-related applications. Inventive in problem solving on a day-to-day basis, mostly thanks to his rich, hands-on experience with Magento, he feels comfortable proposing alternatives to demands he feels can be improved, even when this means pulling a late shift to meet deadlines. He is no stranger when it comes to topics such as payment and shipping gateways, order and invoice functionalities, various third-party ERP, and fulfillment system integrations with Magento. He holds several respected IT certifications such as Zend Certified Engineer, Magento Certified Developer Plus, and JavaScript Certified Developer.

He currently works as a Chief Technology Officer at Inchoo, a Magento Gold Solution partner company that offers top-quality e-commerce solutions, specializing in the Magento e-commerce platform. He was the first person to join Inchoo after Tomislav (CEO) founded it in May 2008, in Osijek, Croatia.

Instant E-Commerce with Magento: Build a Shop by *Packt Publishing* was his first Magento-related book oriented toward Magento newcomers, after which he decided to write this one for developers.

Special thanks in writing this book go toward my understanding family and co-workers who found themselves involved in the process.

About the Reviewers

Matej Krivak is an experienced web/database developer, born and raised in Osijek, Croatia.

He has a Master's degree in Engineering (more specifically, Process Computing) from the Faculty of Electrical Engineering in Osijek where he graduated with highest honors (that is, summa cum laude).

Matej is currently working for Inchoo, a Croatian company specializing in the creation of e-commerce solutions based on Magento, as a team leader and a senior back-end developer. In the past, he has worked for Dialog, a small Croatian company, where he developed and maintained systems based on Oracle technologies.

He has a good knowledge of Magento, Oracle Designer 9*i*/11*g*, and various relational database management systems (for example, MySQL, Oracle, and Microsoft SQL Server).

Andrea De Pirro graduated with a Master's degree in Computer Engineering at Università degli Studi di Roma Tre in Rome. He started his career as a Symfony and Drupal developer at Emoveo, an innovative startup in Rome, learning about Agile methodologies and PHP best practices. His next step was moving to Bioversity International, where he developed and managed a digital asset management project with the Alfresco J2EE platform. Then he moved to Wind, one of the largest Italian mobile operators, developing Java and PHP web services. Finally, he moved to Barcelona, working at Newshore on large e-commerce projects based on Magento and Zend Framework, for customers such as Privalia, Groupalia, and Intercom. Now he's co-founder of Yameveo, a company specializing in e-commerce solutions and web applications.

Alistair Stead is Technical Assurance Manager at Session Digital UK and a Magento Certification board member. Alistair has been developing software with PHP and other technologies since 2000 and has helped many enterprise clients from the UK and Europe realize complex commerce solutions.

He speaks regularly at conferences, not only regarding Magento but also many different technical topics relevant to current development practices, performance, and scalability.

In his spare time you will find Alistair tinkering with new technology and tweeting about the results.

www.PacktPub.com

Support files, eBooks, discount offers and more

You might want to visit www.PacktPub.com for support files and downloads related to your book.

Did you know that Packt offers eBook versions of every book published, with PDF and ePub files available? You can upgrade to the eBook version at www.PacktPub.com and as a print book customer, you are entitled to a discount on the eBook copy. Get in touch with us at service@packtpub.com for more details.

At www.PacktPub.com, you can also read a collection of free technical articles, sign up for a range of free newsletters and receive exclusive discounts and offers on Packt books and eBooks.

PACKTLIB®

http://PacktLib.PacktPub.com

Do you need instant solutions to your IT questions? PacktLib is Packt's online digital book library. Here, you can access, read and search across Packt's entire library of books.

Why Subscribe?

- Fully searchable across every book published by Packt
- Copy and paste, print and bookmark content
- On demand and accessible via web browser

Free Access for Packt account holders

If you have an account with Packt at www.PacktPub.com, you can use this to access PacktLib today and view nine entirely free books. Simply use your login credentials for immediate access.

Table of Contents

Preface

Building Magento extensions can be a challenging task for several reasons. On one side a developer is required to have a solid understanding of advanced PHP object-oriented knowledge, while on the other side there are numerous Magento-specific patterns and configuration options you need to master. This book will give you enough insight into the structure and concepts, and teach you a few tricks that will help you master Magento more easily. By the end of the book, you should familiarize yourself with configuration files, models, blocks, controllers, event/observers, shipping, and payment methods. All of these should form a solid foundation for your developing modules later.

What this book covers

Chapter 1, An Overview of Magento Extensions, introduces you to the overall Magento directory structure, digging all the way down to the individual module structure. Important concepts such as Block, Model, Helper, and controller classes together with configuration files are introduced and explained.

Chapter 2, Building the Extension – Maximum Order Amount, guides you through your first real-world module. Using the event/observer system, you build a simple but powerful module for limiting the amount of maximum purchase.

Chapter 3, Building the Extension – Logger, introduces you to the practical usage of models and installation scripts in Magento, together with the use of administration grids for displaying the entity data.

Chapter 4, Building the Extension – Shipping, introduces you to the Magento shipping methods system, showing you a practical example for building your own shipping method.

Chapter 5, Building the Extension – Payment, introduces you to the Magento payment methods system, showing you a practical example for building your own payment method.

Chapter 6, Packaging and Publishing Your Extension, introduces you to the process of packaging your extension for distribution over the Magento Connect extension marketplace.

What you need for this book

In order to successfully run all the examples provided in this book, you will need either your own web server or third-party web hosting solution. The Magento Community Edition platform itself comes with a detailed list of system requirements, which you can find at `http://www.magentocommerce.com/system-requirements`. If you are able to install Magento on your server, you should be able to follow all the guidelines given in the book.

Who this book is for

This book is primarily intended for intermediate to advanced PHP developers looking for a way into Magento module development. The existing Magento developers might find certain chapters interesting as well, depending on their previous experience.

Conventions

In this book, you will find a number of styles of text that distinguish between different kinds of information. Here are some examples of these styles, and an explanation of their meaning.

Code words in text are shown as follows: "This is basically a `.htaccess` template file used for creating new stores within subfolders."

A block of code is set as follows:

```
<?xml version="1.0"?>
<config>
   <modules>
      <Foggyline_HappyHour>
         <active>true</active>
```

```
            <codePool>community</codePool>
        </Foggyline_HappyHour>
    </modules>
</config>
```

New terms and **important words** are shown in bold. Words that you see on the screen, in menus or dialog boxes for example, appear in the text like this: "You can confirm that by going under the Magento administration under **System** | **Configuration** | **Advanced** | **Advanced** | **Disable Modules Output**."

[Warnings or important notes appear in a box like this.]

[Tips and tricks appear like this.]

Reader feedback

Feedback from our readers is always welcome. Let us know what you think about this book—what you liked or may have disliked. Reader feedback is important for us to develop titles that you really get the most out of.

To send us general feedback, simply send an e-mail to `feedback@packtpub.com`, and mention the book title via the subject of your message.

If there is a topic that you have expertise in and you are interested in either writing or contributing to a book, see our author guide on `www.packtpub.com/authors`.

Customer support

Now that you are the proud owner of a Packt book, we have a number of things to help you to get the most from your purchase.

Downloading the example code

You can download the example code files for all Packt books you have purchased from your account at `http://www.packtpub.com`. If you purchased this book elsewhere, you can visit `http://www.packtpub.com/support` and register to have the files e-mailed directly to you.

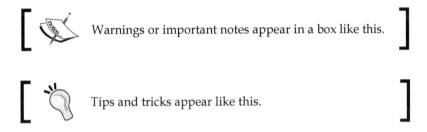

Errata

Although we have taken every care to ensure the accuracy of our content, mistakes do happen. If you find a mistake in one of our books—maybe a mistake in the text or the code—we would be grateful if you would report this to us. By doing so, you can save other readers from frustration and help us improve subsequent versions of this book. If you find any errata, please report them by visiting `http://www.packtpub.com/submit-errata`, selecting your book, clicking on the **errata submission form** link, and entering the details of your errata. Once your errata are verified, your submission will be accepted and the errata will be uploaded on our website, or added to any list of existing errata, under the Errata section of that title. Any existing errata can be viewed by selecting your title from `http://www.packtpub.com/support`.

Piracy

Piracy of copyright material on the Internet is an ongoing problem across all media. At Packt, we take the protection of our copyright and licenses very seriously. If you come across any illegal copies of our works, in any form, on the Internet, please provide us with the location address or website name immediately so that we can pursue a remedy.

Please contact us at `copyright@packtpub.com` with a link to the suspected pirated material.

We appreciate your help in protecting our authors, and our ability to bring you valuable content.

Questions

You can contact us at `questions@packtpub.com` if you are having a problem with any aspect of the book, and we will do our best to address it.

1
An Overview of Magento Extensions

Creating Magento extensions can be an extremely challenging and time-consuming task depending on several factors such as your knowledge of Magento internals, overall development skills, and the complexity of the extension functionality itself. Having a deep insight into Magento internals, its structure, and accompanying tips and tricks will provide you with a strong foundation for clean and unobtrusive Magento extension development.

The word unobtrusive should be a constant thought throughout your entire development process. The reason is simple; given the massiveness of the Magento platform, it is way too easy to build extensions that clash with other third-party extensions. This is usually a beginner's flaw, which we will hopefully avoid once we have finished reading this book. The examples listed in this book are targeted toward Magento Community Edition 1.7.0.2. Version 1.7.0.2 is the last stable release at the time of writing.

You can download the full installation archive from the official Magento site at `http://www.magentocommerce.com`. You might need to register as a user on a site in order to initiate the download.

The root directory structure

Once you download the full release and set up your work environment, you should see a root Magento folder structure with the following files and folders in it:

- **Folders**: app, downloader, errors, includes, js, lib, media, pkginfo, shell, skin, and var
- **Files**: .htaccess, cron.sh,.htaccess.sample, LICENSE.html, mage, LICENSE.txt, favicon.ico, LICENSE_AFL.txt, get.php php.ini.sample, RELEASE_NOTES.txt, api.php, index.php, index.php.sample, cron.php, and install.php

Throughout this book we will be referencing our URL examples as if they are executing on the magento.loc domain. You are free to set your local Apache virtual host and host file to any domain you prefer, as long as you keep this in mind. If you're hearing about virtual host terminology for the first time, please refer to the Apache Virtual Host documentation at http://httpd.apache.org/docs/2.4/vhosts/.

Here is a quick summary of each of those files and folders:

- .htaccess: This file is a directory-level configuration file supported by several web servers, most notably the Apache web server. It controls mod_rewrite for fancy URLs and sets configuration server variables (such as memory limit) and PHP maximum execution time.
- .htaccess.sample: This is basically a .htaccess template file used for creating new stores within subfolders.
- api.php: This is primarily used for the Magento REST API, but can be used for SOAP and XML-RPC API server functionality as well.
- app: This is where you will find Magento core code files for the backend and for the frontend. This folder is basically the heart of the Magento platform. Later on, we will dive into this folder for more details, given that this is the folder that you as an extension developer will spend most of your time on.
- cron.php: This file, when triggered via URL or via console PHP, will trigger certain Magento cron jobs logic.
- cron.sh: This file is a Unix shell script version of cron.php.

- `downloader`: This folder is used by the Magento Connect Manager, which is the functionality you access from the Magento administration area by navigating to **System** | **Magento Connect** | **Magento Connect Manager**.
- `errors`: This folder is a host for a slightly separate Magento functionality, the one that jumps in with error handling when your Magento store gets an exception during code execution.
- `favicon.ico`: This is your standard 16 x 16 px website icon.
- `get.php`: This file hosts a feature that allows core media files to be stored and served from the database. With the Database File Storage system in place, Magento would redirect requests for media files to `get.php`.
- `includes`: This folder is used by the `Mage_Compiler` extension whose functionality can be accessed via Magento administration **System** | **Tools** | **Compilation**. The idea behind the Magento compiler feature is that you end up with a PHP system that pulls all of its classes from one folder, thus, giving it a massive performance boost.
- `index.php`: This is a main entry point to your application, the main loader file for Magento, and the file that initializes everything. Every request for every Magento page goes through this file.
- `index.php.sample`: This file is just a backup copy of the `index.php` file.
- `js`: This folder holds the core Magento JavaScript libraries, such as Prototype, scriptaculous.js, ExtJS, and a few others, some of which are from Magento itself.
- `lib`: This folder holds the core Magento PHP libraries, such as 3DSecure, Google Checkout, phpseclib, Zend, and a few others, some of which are from Magento itself.
- `LICENSE*`: These are the Magento licence files in various formats (`LICENSE_AFL.txt`, `LICENSE.html`, and `LICENSE.txt`).
- `mage`: This is a Magento Connect command-line tool. It allows you to add/remove channels, install and uninstall packages (extensions), and various other package-related tasks.
- `media`: This folder contains all the media files, mostly just images from various products, categories, and CMS pages.
- `php.ini.sample`: This file is a sample `php.ini` file for PHP CGI/FastCGI installations. Sample files are not actually used by the Magento application.
- `pkginfo`: This folder contains text files that largely operate as debug files to inform us about changes when extensions are upgraded in any way.

- `RELEASE_NOTES.txt`: This file contains the release notes and changes for various Magento versions, starting from version 1.4.0.0 and later.
- `shell`: This folder contains several PHP-based shell tools, such as compiler, indexer, and logger.
- `skin`: This folder contains various CSS and JavaScript files specific for individual Magento themes. Files in this folder and its subfolder go hand in hand with files in `app/design` folder, as these two locations actually result in one fully featured Magento theme or package.
- `var`: This folder contains sessions, logs, reports, configuration cache, lock files for application processes, and possible various other files distributed among individual subfolders. During development, you can freely select all the subfolders and delete them, as Magento will recreate all of them on the next page request. From a standpoint of a Magento extension developer, you might find yourself looking into the `var/log` and `var/report` folders every now and then.

Now that we have covered the basic root folder structure, it's time to dig deeper into the most used folder of all, the `app` folder, as shown in the following diagram:

```
app/
├── Mage.php
├── code
│   ├── community
│   │   └── Phoenix
│   │       └── Moneybookers
│   └── core
│       ├── Mage
│       └── Zend
├── design
│   ├── adminhtml
│   ├── frontend
│   │   ├── base
│   │   │   └── default
│   │   │       ├── etc
│   │   │       ├── layout
│   │   │       └── template
│   │   └── default
│   │       ├── blank
│   │       ├── default
│   │       ├── iphone
│   │       └── modern
│   └── install
├── etc
```

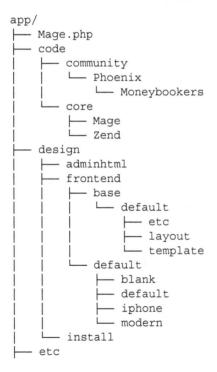

```
|   ├── config.xml
|   ├── local.xml.additional
|   ├── local.xml.template
|   └── modules
└── local
    └── en_US
```

Code pools

The folder `code` is a placeholder for what is called a **codePool** in Magento. Usually, there are three code pools in Magento, that is, three subfolders: `community`, `core`, and `local`.

The folder `local` is sometimes missing from the downloaded installation archive, as it is empty by default.

Let's take a deeper look at the community codePool for the default Magento installation as shown in the following diagram:

```
community/
└── Phoenix
    └── Moneybookers
        ├── Block
        |   ├── Form.php
        |   ├── ...
        |   └── Redirect.php
        ├── Helper
        |   └── Data.php
        ├── Model
        |   ├── Abstract.php
        |   ├── ...
        |   └── Wlt.php
        ├── controllers
        |   ├── MoneybookersController.php
        |   └── ProcessingController.php
        ├── etc
        |   ├── config.xml
        |   └── system.xml
        └── sql
            └── moneybookers_setup
                ├── install-1.6.0.0.php
                └── mysql4-upgrade-1.2-1.2.0.1.php
```

Here, the Phoenix folder is what is called the vendor namespace, and it usually matches your company identifier or something else unique to you. Within the Phoenix folder there is a Moneybookers subfolder that stands for your actual extension name.

To summarize, the formula for your extension code location should be something like app/code/community/YourNamespace/YourModuleName/ or app/code/local/YourNamespace/YourModuleName/.

There is a simple rule as to whether to choose community or local codePool:

- Choose the community codePool for extensions that you plan to share across projects, or possibly upload to Magento Connect
- Choose the local codePool for extensions that are specific for the project you are working on and won't be shared with the public

For example, let's imagine that our company name is Foggyline and the extension we are building is called Happy Hour. As we wish to share our extension with the community, we can put it into a folder such as app/code/community/Foggyline/HappyHour/.

All the Magento core code is also divided into extensions, and is located under the app/code/core/Mage folder. You should never place any of your code or edit any of the existing code under the app/code/core folder.

Let us get back to our example from the previous listing, the Moneybookers extension. We can see that it has several subfolders within it:

- Block: This folder contains various PHP classes. You can think of the Block folder as a placeholder for class objects that visually manifest themselves to the user on a frontend. Most of these PHP classes extend the Mage_Core_Block_Template class from within the app/code/core/Mage/Core/Block/Template.php file. These PHP classes are then linked to various layouts and template *.phtml files within the given theme under the app/design folder.
- controllers: This folder contains various PHP classes. You can think of controllers as a glue between our URL actions, models, blocks, and views. Most of these classes extend the Mage_Core_Controller_Front_Action class from within the app/code/core/Mage/Core/Controller/Front/Action.php file or the Mage_Adminhtml_Controller_Action class from within the app/code/core/Mage/Adminhtml/Controller/Action.php file.
- etc: This folder contains various XML configuration files such as adminhtml.xml, api.xml, config.xml, system.xml, wsdl.xml, wsdl2.xml, and wsi.xml. Depending on what type of extension you are building, you might find some configuration files used more than the others.

- `Helper`: This folder contains various PHP classes, most of which extend the `Mage_Core_Helper_Abstract` class from within the `app/code/core/Mage/Core/Helper/Abstract.php` file. The `Helper` classes contain various utility methods that will allow you to perform common tasks.
- `Model`: This folder contains various PHP classes that usually, but not necessarily, represent an entity in a database. This is the folder where you would place most of your business logic.
- `sql`: This folder contains one or more PHP files representing the installer code to be executed during the installation of the extension.

With that said, we will temporarily conclude our trip to the `app/code` folder structure and move on to the `app/etc/modules` folder.

This folder is basically a starting point for every Magento extension. The following listing shows the default content of the `app/etc/modules` folder for the default Magento installation, which is a collection of XML files:

- `Mage_All.xml`
- `Mage_Downloadable.xml`
- `Mage_Api.xml`
- `Mage_ImportExport.xml`
- `Mage_Api2.xml`
- `Mage_Oauth.xml`
- `Mage_Authorizenet.xml`
- `Mage_PageCache.xml`
- `Mage_Bundle.xml`
- `Mage_Persistent.xml`
- `Mage_Captcha.xml`
- `Mage_Weee.xml`
- `Mage_Centinel.xml`
- `Mage_Widget.xml`
- `Mage_Compiler.xml`
- `Mage_XmlConnect.xml`
- `Mage_Connect.xml`
- `Phoenix_Moneybookers.xml`
- `Mage_CurrencySymbol.xml`

For example, if we were to create our `Foggyline/Happy Hour` extension, we would need to create a file `app/etc/modules/Foggyline_HappyHour.xml` as we will show later on.

Next, we move onto the `app/local` folder. This is where the translation files reside. If you were building an extension that would support multiple languages, for example English and German, you might want to create the following files:

- `app/locale/en_US/Foggyline_HappyHour.csv`
- `app/locale/de_DE/Foggyline_HappyHour.csv`

The exact filename in this case does not have to be `Foggyline_HappyHour.csv`; this is something that is set by you within the extension configuration.

The theme system

In order to successfully build extensions that visually manifest themselves to the user either on the backend or frontend, we need to get familiar with the theme system. The theme system is comprised of two distributed parts: one found under the `app/design` folder and the other under the root `skin` folder. Files found under the `app/design` folder are PHP template files and XML layout configuration files. Within the PHP template files you can find the mix of HTML, PHP, and some JavaScript.

The structure of the app/design folder is shown in the following diagram:

```
app/
├── design
│   ├── adminhtml
│   ├── frontend
│   │   ├── base
│   │   │   └── default
│   │   │       ├── etc
│   │   │       ├── layout
│   │   │       └── template
│   │   └── default
│   │       ├── blank
│   │       ├── default
│   │       ├── iphone
│   │       └── modern
│   └── install
```

There are three main subfolders here as follows:

- `adminhtml`: This folder contains the XML layouts and PHTML view files used for rendering the Magento administration area, the area that the admin user sees

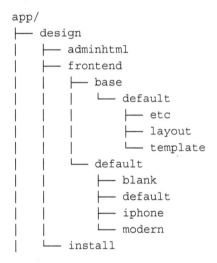

- `frontend`: This folder contains the XML layouts and PHTML view files used for rendering the Magento frontend area, the area that the customers see.
- `install`: This folder contains the XML layouts and PHTML view files used for rendering the Magento installation process

Once you step into one of them you should see a list of so called packages.

For example, stepping into the frontend shows two packages available, `base` and `default`. Drilling down into individual packages, come themes. For example, the package `default` has four themes in it: `blank`, `default`, `iphone`, and `modern`. By default, once you install the Magento package the initial active theme is default within the `default` package.

You will often hear about the frontend developer using a shorthand when talking about theme; for example, if they say `default/hello`, it would mean the `default` package with the theme named `hello`.

There is one important thing to know about Magento themes; they have a fallback mechanism; for example, if someone in the administration interface sets the configuration to use a theme called hello from the `default` package; and if the theme is missing, for example, the `app/design/frontend/default/hello/template/catalog/product/view.phtml` file in its structure, Magento will use `app/design/frontend/default/default/template/catalog/product/view.phtml` from the `default` theme; and if that file is missing as well, Magento will fall back to the `base` package for the `app/design/frontend/base/default/template/catalog/product/view.phtml` file.

We won't get into the details of Magento design packages and themes. There is plenty to be said about this topic that could fit into a new book. For the purpose of this book, there are a few things that you need to know as a Magento extension developer in terms of writing unobtrusive extensions.

Firstly, all your layout and view files should go under the `/app/design/frontend/defaultdefault/default` directory.

Secondly, you should never overwrite the existing `.xml` layout or template `.phtml` file from within the `/app/design/frontend/default/default` directory, rather create your own. For example, imagine you are doing some product image switcher extension, and you conclude that you need to do some modifications to the `app/design/frontend/default/default/template/catalog/product/view/media.phtml` file. A more valid approach would be to create a proper XML layout update file with handles rewriting the `media.phtml` usage to, let's say, `media_product_image_switcher.phtml`.

This might not make much sense for you now; but once you get your head around layout updates, the idea will be pretty clear. We will now temporarily conclude our trip to the `app/design` folder structure and move on to the root `skin` folder. The structure of the `skin` folder is similar to that of `app/design`, as shown in the following diagram:

```
skin/
├── adminhtml
├── frontend
│   ├── base
│   │   └── default
│   │       ├── css
│   │       ├── favicon.ico
│   │       ├── images
│   │       ├── js
│   │       └── lib
│   │           └── prototype
│   └── default
│       ├── blank
│       ├── blue
│       ├── default
│       │   ├── css
│       │   ├── favicon.ico
│       │   └── images
│       ├── french
│       ├── german
│       ├── iphone
│       └── modern
└── install
```

There is not much to say about the `skin` folder. It's a placeholder for all your theme-specific CSS, JavaScript, and image files. If you are developing community-distributed extensions, it makes sense to reduce the usage of CSS to absolute minimum, if any, in your extension. The reason is that you cannot know which theme the user will use and how your extension visual components design will impact its theme.

The same thing cannot be said for JavaScript, as you will most likely notice yourself if you keep developing a lot of community extensions. Adding your custom JavaScript code to a `skin/frontend/default/default/js` folder is a nice, clean, and unobtrusive way of doing it. As the skin folder has the same fallback functionality as the `app/design` folder, you do not need to know upfront the theme that the user will use.

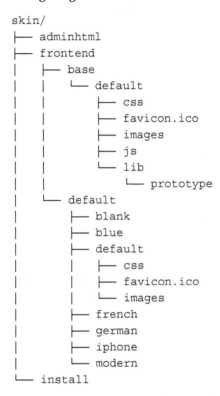

Later on, as you sharpen your Magento developer skills you might ask yourself, "Why not use the root `js` folder to add your JavaScript code?" Technically, you could, and it would be perfectly valid; no tricks or hacks in that approach. However, the root `js` folder should be looked upon as a third-party JavaScript library container, while the `skin/frontend/default/default/js` folder should be looked upon as your custom JavaScript extension-related code container. For example, it makes no sense to place your product image switcher extension JavaScript into the root `js` folder if it's a JavaScript code that works only with your extension and is not intended for general re-use.

With this we can conclude the relevant Magento folder structure that you as a Magento extension developer should be familiar with. In general, these five locations should be all to build fully functional, clean, and unobtrusive extensions:

- `app/etc/modules/` - required
- `app/locale/` - optional
- `app/code/community/YourNamespace/YourModuleName/` - required
- `/app/design/frontend/default/default/` (or `/app/design/adminhtml/default/default/ for backend area`) - optional
- `skin/frontend/default/default/` (or `skin/adminhtml/default/default/`) - optional

Depending on the complexity and the functionality your extension tries to fulfill, you might end up using just a few or all of these directory locations within a single extension.

Basic extension configuration

With everything said, by now we should have a solid understanding of the Magento directory structure and be ready to grasp further concepts of the Magento internal structure.

What better way to explain things than an example; so let's start off by creating the simplest extension, which we will then extend bit by bit as we explain the Magento way of doing the object-oriented **Model-View-Controller** (**MVC**) architecture. If you are hearing of MVC for the first time, please take some time to familiarize yourself with the concept. You can find good starting material about it at `http://en.wikipedia.org/wiki/Model-view-controller`.

Previously, we gave examples on the extension name `Foggyline_HappyHour`, so let's start with that.

In Magento, everything starts with a configuration file; after all, Magento is what we call the configuration-based MVC system. In a configuration-based system, in addition to adding the new files and classes, you often need to explicitly tell the system about them.

The first file we will create is `app/etc/modules/Foggyline_HappyHour.xml` with the following content:

```
<?xml version="1.0"?>
<config>
    <modules>
        <Foggyline_HappyHour>
            <active>true</active>
                <codePool>community</codePool>
        </Foggyline_HappyHour>
    </modules>
</config>
```

With this file in place, Magento already becomes aware of your extension. You can confirm that by going under the Magento administration under **System | Configuration | Advanced | Advanced | Disable Modules Output**. Once you're there, you should see your `Foggyline_HappyHour` extension on the list. It is important to know that setting the **Disable Modules Output** value to **Disabled** and saving the configuration has absolutely no impact on your extension being truly enabled or disabled.

Disabling the extension output is not the same as disabling the extension itself. Disabling the output of the extension via this configuration option has an effect only on your extension block classes that represent the visually output part of your extension. To truly disable the extension, one must edit the `app/etc/modules/Foggyline_HappyHour.xml` file and change `<active>true</active>` to `<active>false</active>`.

Now that Magento sees our extension, we move on to the next step: creating the `app/code/community/Foggyline/HappyHour/etc/config.xml` file. This `config.xml` file is what is usually referred to as the extension configuration file by developers. The following code is the basic definition of our `app/code/community/Foggyline/HappyHour/etc/config.xml` file:

```
<?xml version="1.0"?>
<config>
    <modules>
```

```
        <Foggyline_HappyHour>
            <version>1.0.0.0</version>
        </Foggyline_HappyHour>
    </modules>
</config>
```

Controllers

By itself, the content of the `app/code/community/Foggyline/HappyHour/etc/config.xml` file won't have any additional effect on Magento, so let's move on to extending our extension. First, we will create a controller in order to output Hello World to the browser. To do this, we need to add the `routers` definition in `frontend` to our `config.xml` file.

```
<?xml version="1.0"?>"?>
<config>
<!-- … other elements ... -->
    <frontend>
        <routers>
            <foggyline_happyhour>
                <use>standard</use>
                    <args>
                        <module>Foggyline_HappyHour</module>
                        <frontName>happyhour</frontName>
                    </args>
            </foggyline_happyhour>
        </routers>
    </frontend>
<!-- … other elements ... -->
</config>
```

The `frontend` tag refers to a Magento area. Magento has three distinctive areas: frontend, admin, and install. The frontend area is what your customers see, the public facing shopping cart. The admin area is what your Magento admin users see, the administrative interface. The install area is what you see the very first time you install Magento, the installation process.

The `routers` tag encloses the configuration information about routers.

The `frontName` tag is sort of an alias for the desired route we want Magento to react to.

When a router parses a URL, it gets separated as follows: `http://example.com/frontName/actionControllerName/actionMethod/`. By defining a value of `happyhour` in the `<frontName>` tag, we're telling Magento that we want the system to respond to URLs in the form of `http://example.com/happyhour/*`.

It's important to understand that frontName and the Front Controller object are not the same thing.

The foggyline_happyhour tag should be the lowercase version of your extension name. Our extension name is Foggyline_HappyHour; this tag is foggyline_happyhour.

The extension tag should be the full name of your extension, including its namespace/extensionname name. This will be used by the system to locate your controller files.

Now we need to create a controller file. The module controller files are stored under the controllers subfolder. So let's create an app/code/community/Foggyline/HappyHour/controllers/HelloController.php class file with the following content:

```
<?php

class Foggyline_HappyHour_HelloController extends Mage_Core_
Controller_Front_Action
{
    public function helloWorldAction()
    {
        echo 'Hello World #1.';
    }
}
```

Once you are done, you can try opening the following URL in the browser: http://magento.loc/index.php/happyhour/hello/helloWorld. You should be able to see the Hello World #1. message. The URL path is constructed from your config.xml router frontName, the controller name itself, and the controller action name. There are two main types of controllers in Magento:

- frontend: This contains all the controller classes that extend (derive from) the Mage_Core_Controller_Front_Action class
- backend / admin: This contains all the controller classes that extend (derive from) the Mage_Adminhtml_Controller_Action class

URLs for admin controller actions can only be accessed if you are logged in to the Magento administration interface.

Blocks

Looking within the `helloWorldAction()` method, you can see a call towards the `createBlock()` method with the string `'core/text'` as a parameter. Where does `'core/text'` come from and what does it mean? In order to understand that, we will further extend our `config.xml` file by adding a `blocks` element to it as follows:

```
<?xml version="1.0"?>
<config>
<!-- … other elements ... -->
   <global>
      <blocks>
         <foggyline_happyhour>
            <class>Foggyline_HappyHour_Block</class>
         </foggyline_happyhour>
      </blocks>
   </global>
<!-- … other elements ... -->
</config>
```

The element `foggyline_happyhour` is known as the class group. The element `foggyline_happyhour` is a class group name and its inner class element is basically a shortcut for your extensions `Block` type PHP classes. For example, the following is a modified code for our `helloWorldAction()` method shown previously:

```
<?php

class Foggyline_HappyHour_HelloController extends Mage_Core_
Controller_Front_Action
{
   public function helloWorldAction()
   {
      $this->loadLayout();

      $block = $this->getLayout()->createBlock('foggyline_happyhour/
hello');
      $block->setText('Hello World #2.');

      $this->getLayout()->getBlock('content')->insert($block);

      $this->renderLayout();
   }
}
```

You can see that we are no longer calling the `createBlock()` method with `'core/text'` but with the `'foggyline_happyhour/hello'` parameter. This is like telling Magento to load the hello class (the `Hello.php` file) that can be found under the classpath mapped by the `foggyline_happyhour` class group. As the `foggyline_happyhour` class group has its class value set to `Foggyline_HappyHour_Block`, Magento expects to find the `app/code/community/Foggyline/HappyHour/Block/Hello.php` file.

How and why exactly does Magento expect the `Hello.php` file to be at a certain location? The answer to this lies in a robust autoloading functionality of the Magento system based on a configuration and file naming convention. You can split all Magento classes into four parts that we'll call the vendor namespace, extension name, class group, and filename itself.

The vendor namespace helps us prevent name collisions between extensions, letting you know which extension is the owner of the class. For example, all core Magento extensions use the `mage` namespace.

The module name plays a crucial part in the autoloading system. All the proper customization of Magento is done through individual extensions.

The class group is a sort of alias defined within the extension's configuration file, an alias towards a class folder within the extension directory. There are several main types of class groups, such as the one for `Model`, `Block`, `Helper`.

Finally, the name of the file itself. Each class should have a unique name within a class group that describes its intended use or function.

Magento's autoloading functionality uses these parts to determine where to find the source for a given class as shown in the following example: `VendorNamespace/ModuleName/ClassGroup/FileName.php`.

Go ahead and create the file `Hello.php` with the following content:

```
<?php

class Foggyline_HappyHour_Block_Hello extends Mage_Core_Block_Text
{

}
```

Now that you have modified `helloWorldAction()` and created the `Hello.php` class file, go ahead and open the `http://magento.loc/index.php/happyhour/hello/helloWorld` URL in the browser. The result should be the same as in the previous case; you should be able to see the fully loaded Magento page with the **Hello World #2.** message shown under the content area.

Our `Hello` block class extends `Mage_Core_Block_Text`. However, chances are that most of the time you will be extending the `Mage_Core_Block_Template` class, where your `Hello` block class might look like something as follows:

```
<?php

class Foggyline_HappyHour_Block_Hello extends Mage_Core_Block_Template
{
   public function __construct()
   {
      parent::__construct();
      $this->setTemplate('foggyline_happyhour/hello.phtml');
   }
}
```

The difference between extending `Mage_Core_Block_Text` or `Mage_Core_Block_Template` is that the latter requires you to define a view `*.phtml` file under the `theme` folder, and thus, is more designer friendly. In order for it to successfully work, you need to create the `app/design/frontend/default/default/template/foggyline_happyhour/hello.phtml` or `app/design/frontend/base/default/template/foggyline_happyhour/hello.phtml` file. You might find the latter to be a safer location for your view files, as it is not dependent on your customer theme and package settings. Thus, the Magento theme fallback mechanism will always pick it up. Now if you put your `Hello World #3.` string within the `hello.phtml` file and then re-open the `http://magento.loc/index.php/happyhour/hello/helloWorld` URI in your browser, you should again see the fully loaded Magento page with the **Hello World #3.** message shown under the content area. Our goal here is to give you the basics of functional extension, so we will now leave the controllers and blocks behind and move to the model.

> **Downloading the example code**
>
> You can download the example code files for all Packt books you have purchased from your account at http://www.packtpub.com. If you purchased this book elsewhere, you can visit http://www.packtpub.com/supportand register to have the files e-mailed directly to you.

The model, resource, and collection

A model represents the data for the better part, and to a certain extent a business logic of your application. Models in Magento take the **Object Relational Mapping** (**ORM**) approach, thus having the developer to strictly deal with objects while their data is then automatically persisted to the database. If you are hearing about ORM for the first time, please take some time to familiarize yourself with the concept; you can find good starting material about it at `http://en.wikipedia.org/wiki/Object-relational_mapping`. Theoretically, you could write and execute raw SQL queries in Magento. However, doing so is not advised, especially if you plan on distributing your extensions.

There are two types of models in Magento:

- **Basic Data Model**: This is a simpler model type, sort of like an Active Record pattern-based model. If you're hearing about Active Record for the first time, please take some time to familiarize yourself with the concept; you can find good starting material about it at `https://en.wikipedia.org/wiki/Active_record_pattern`.
- **EAV (Entity-Attribute-Value) Data Model**: This is a complex model type, which enables you to dynamically create new attributes on an entity. As EAV Data Model is significantly more complex than Basic Data Model and Basic Data Model will suffice for most of the time, we will focus on Basic Data Model and everything important surrounding it. Each data model you plan to persist to the database, that means models that present an entity, needs to have four files in order for it to work fully:
    - **The model file**: This extends the `Mage_Core_Model_Abstract` class. This represents single entity, its properties (fields), and possible business logic within it.
    - **The model resource file**: This extends the `Mage_Core_Model_Resource_Db_Abstract` class. This is your connection to the database; think of it as the thing that saves your entity properties (fields) database.
    - **The model collection file**: This extends the `Mage_Core_Model_Resource_Db_Collection_Abstract` class. This is your collection of several entities, a collection that can be filtered, sorted, and manipulated.
    - **The installation script file**: In its simplest definition this is the PHP file through which you, in an object-oriented way, create your database table(s).

For our example, we will go ahead and create our extensions `User` model. The first thing we need to do is to set up its configuration within the `config.xml` file as follows:

```
<?xml version="1.0"?>
<config>
   <global>
<!-- … other elements ... -->
      <models>
         <foggyline_happyhour>
            <class>Foggyline_HappyHour_Model</class>
            <resourceModel>foggyline_happyhour_resource</
resourceModel>
         </foggyline_happyhour>
         <foggyline_happyhour_resource>
            <class>Foggyline_HappyHour_Model_Resource</class>
            <entities>
               <user>
                  <table>foggyline_happyhour_user</table>
               </user>
            </entities>
         </foggyline_happyhour_resource>
      </models>
      <resources>
         <foggyline_happyhour_setup>
            <setup>
               <model>Foggyline_HappyHour</model>
            </setup>
         </foggyline_happyhour_setup>
      </resources>
<!-- … other elements ... -->
   </global>
</config>
```

The amount of new elements added to XML might look a bit discouraging, try not to get frightened by it. Let's break it down:

- The element `foggyline_happyhour` contains our class group model definition, which actually tells Magento that our Model PHP class files can be found under our extensions directory `app/code/community/Foggyline/HappyHour/Model/`. Further, the `foggyline_happyhour` element contains the resourceModel element whose value points further to the element `foggyline_happyhour_resource`.

- The element `foggyline_happyhour_resource` contains our class group model resource definition, which actually tells Magento that our Model Resource PHP class files can be found under our extensions directory `app/code/community/Foggyline/HappyHour/Model/Resource/`. Further, the `foggyline_happyhour_resource` element contains the entities element that is a list of all our entities and their mapped database table names.
- The element `foggyline_happyhour_setup` contains the setup definition for our extension. There is a lot more you can define here, which is not visible in our example due to simplicity. For example, we could have defined completely different read / write database connections here, specific to our extension. The most important thing to keep in mind here, however, is the following: the element name `foggyline_happyhour_setup` must match the folder name for your installation script `app/code/community/Foggyline/HappyHour/sql/foggyline_happyhour_setup/`.

Now let us create the four files required for our extensions model entity to work fully.

First we will create a model file `app/code/community/Foggyline/HappyHour/Model/User.php` with the following content:

```
<?php

class Foggyline_HappyHour_Model_User extends Mage_Core_Model_Abstract
{
   protected $_eventPrefix      = 'foggyline_happyhour_user';
   protected $_eventObject      = 'user';

   protected function _construct()
   {
      $this->_init('foggyline_happyhour/user');
   }
}
```

All basic data models, such as our `Foggyline_HappyHour_Model_User`, should extend the `Mage_Core_Model_Abstract` class. This abstract class forces you to implement a single method named `_construct`. Please note that this is not PHP's constructor `__construct`.

The `_construct` method should call the extending class' `_init` method with the same identifying URI you will be using in the `Mage::getModel` method call. Also, note the class-protected properties `$_eventPrefix` and `$_eventObject`. It is highly recommended, although not required, for you to define these properties. Values of both the properties can be freely assigned; however, you should follow your extension-naming scheme here as shown earlier.

Once we get to the Magento event/observer system later in the chapters, the meaning of these properties and how they make your code extendible by third-party developers will become more clear.

Every model has its own resource class. When a model in Magento needs to talk to the database, Magento will make the following method call to get the model resource `Mage::getResourceModel('class_group/modelname');`. Without resource classes, models would not be able to write to the database. Having that in mind, we create the model resource file `app/code/community/Foggyline/HappyHour/Model/Resource/User.php` with the following content:

```
<?php

class Foggyline_HappyHour_Model_Resource_User extends Mage_Core_Model_
Resource_Db_Abstract
{
    protected function _construct()
    {
        $this->_init('foggyline_happyhour/user', 'user_id');
    }
}
```

Again, we have the same pattern: the construct method should call the extending class' `init` method with the same identifying URI, with a slight exception of the existing second parameter in this case, which matches the primary key column name in the database. So in this case, the string `user_id` matches the primary key column name in the database.

Finally, we address the model collection file. As Magento does not like juggling its model objects through plain PHP arrays, it defines a unique collection object associated with each model. Collection objects implement the PHP IteratorAggregate and Countable interfaces, which means they can be passed to the count function and used for each constructs.

We create the model collection file `app/code/community/Foggyline/HappyHour/Model/Resource/User/Collection.php` with the following content:

```
<?php

class Foggyline_HappyHour_Model_Resource_User_Collection extends Mage_
Core_Model_Resource_Db_Collection_Abstract
{
   public function _construct()
   {
      $this->_init('foggyline_happyhour/user');
   }
}
```

Just as we did with our other classes we define the construct method, which calls the extending class' `init` method with the same identifying URI.

Finally, we create an installation script file `app/code/community/Foggyline/HappyHour/sql/foggyline_happyhour_setup/install-1.0.0.0.php` with the following content:

```
<?php

/* @var $installer Mage_Core_Model_Resource_Setup */
$installer = $this;

$installer->startSetup();

$table = $installer->getConnection()
   ->newTable($installer->getTable('foggyline_happyhour/user'))
   ->addColumn('user_id', Varien_Db_Ddl_Table::TYPE_INTEGER, null,
array(
      'identity'  => true,
      'unsigned'  => true,
      'nullable'  => false,
      'primary'   => true,
      ), 'Id')
   ->addColumn('firstname', Varien_Db_Ddl_Table::TYPE_VARCHAR, null,
array(
      'nullable'  => false,
      ), 'User first name')
   ->addColumn('lastname', Varien_Db_Ddl_Table::TYPE_VARCHAR, null,
array(
      'nullable'  => false,
      ), 'User last name')
```

```
    ->setComment('Foggyline_HappyHour User Entity');

$installer->getConnection()->createTable($table);

$installer->endSetup();
```

There is one thing we need to pay special attention to here, the naming of the `install-1.0.0.0.php` file. The number `1.0.0.0` must be equal to the numbers placed under the version element value, or else Magento won't trigger your installation script.

Ever since version 1.6, Magento (in theory) supports more database backends than only MySQL. Thus, technically, the meaning of code within this install script may vary from database to database depending on the implementation.

Given that MySQL is still the default and far more dominant database backend for Magento, it is worth noting what actually goes on behind this installation script. It starts by calling `$installer->startSetup()`, which internally sets `SQL_MODE` to `NO_AUTO_VALUE_ON_ZERO`, and `FOREIGN_KEY_CHECKS` to `0`. The call to `$installer->startSetup()`, on the other hand restores the two mentioned values to their previous states. The rest of the code that lies in between is responsible for the actual table definition and creation.

In our preceding example, we defined a table that will be named `foggyline_happyhour_user`, and three columns named `user_id`, `firstname`, and `lastname`.

These four files conclude our requirement for a fully persistent entity model. In order to check if everything is functioning, load any Magento URL in the browser and then take a look at the database. If the extension is installed correctly, there should be two changes to the database:

- The table `core_resource` should contain an entry with the column code value `foggyline_happyhour_setup` and column version value `1.0.0.0`.
- The table `foggyline_happyhour_user` should have been successfully created in the database with all the columns as defined within the `install-1.0.0.0.php` file.

Note, if you experience issues with your installation script during their execution, such as breaking up due to invalid instructions, be sure to remove the `core_resource` table entry that your extension might have created. After that, simply open the browser and reload any web page from your shop; this will trigger the installation process again.

Now that we have successfully created single entity (`User`) model file, we need to make sure it's working. We can do so by going back to our `Foggyline_HappyHour_HelloController` class and adding the following action to it:

```
<?php

class Foggyline_HappyHour_HelloController extends Mage_Core_
Controller_Front_Action
{
  /* … other code … */
   public function testUserSaveAction()
   {
      $user = Mage::getModel('foggyline_happyhour/user');

      $user->setFirstname('John');
       /* or: $user->setData('firstname', 'John'); */

      $user->setLastname('Doe');
      /* or: $user->setDatata('lastname', 'Doe'); */

      try {
         $user->save();
         echo 'Successfully saved user.';
      } catch (Exception $e) {
         echo $e->getMessage();
         Mage::logException($e);
/* oror: Mage::log($e->getTraceAsString(), null, 'exception.log',
true); */
      }
   }
  /* … other code … */
}
```

Models in Magento get called (instantiated) all across the code. Instantiating the model class is done by the statement `$model = Mage::getModel('classGroup/modelClassName);` which can be seen in the preceding code.

What confuses most of the Magento newcomers is the fact that our model class `Foggyline_HappyHour_Model_User` has absolutely no methods defined other than `_construct()`, which is not the default PHP construct (`__construct()`).

So how is it then that the statements such as `$user->setLastname('Doe');` work? The answer lies in the derived from the `Varien_Object` class found in the `lib/Varien/Object.php` file. One of the things `Varien_Object` provides is Magento's famous getter and setter methods. If you study the class code, you will see that Magento actually uses the class `protected $_data` property internally via the help of PHP magic methods. Executing `$user->setLastname('Doe');` actually sets `$_data['username'] = 'Doe';`. Or to put it differently, it would virtually create a property named `'username'` with the value `'Doe'` on a `$user` object instance.

The same logic goes for setting values. Executing a statement such as `$user->setData('firstname', 'John');` does almost the same as the previous example.

The difference between the two is that `setData()` directly changes the value on the protected `$_data['username']` property, while `setLastname('Doe');` will first try to look for the `setLastname()` method within the `Foggyline_HappyHour_Model_User` class. If the method is found, the value is passed to the method and the method is in charge of passing the value to the protected `$_data['username']` property, possibly doing some modifications on it.

You should take some time to study the inner workings of the `Varien_Object` class, as it is the base class for all of your models.

To continue with our preceding example, if you now try to open the URL `http://magento1702ce.loc/index.php/happyhour/hello/testUserSave` in your browser, you should be able to see the **Successfully saved user** message.

Once you confirm that the entity save action is working, you should test and confirm that the model collection is working too. Create a new action under the `Foggyline_HappyHour_HelloController` class as follows:

```
<?php

class Foggyline_HappyHour_HelloController extends Mage_Core_
Controller_Front_Action
{
   /* … other code … */
   public function testUserCollectionAction()
   {
      $users = Mage::getModel('foggyline_happyhour/user')
           ->getCollection();

      foreach ($users as $user) {
         $firstname = $user->getFirstname();
```

```
            /* or: $user->getData('firstname') */

            $lastname = $user->getLastname();
            /* or: $user->getData('lastname') */

            echo "$firstname $lastname<br />";
        }
    }
    /* ... other code ... */
}
```

If you now try to open the URL `http://magento.loc/index.php/happyhour/hello/testUserCollection` in your browser, you should be able to see the list of your users within the `foggyline_happyhour_user` database table.

If you were able to follow up and all went well, you should now have a fully working model entity. There is a lot more to be said about models; however, this is enough to get you started.

The event/observer pattern

Next, we will move on to an event/observer pattern implemented by Magento. Events and observers are extremely important in Magento because they enable you to easily hook onto various parts of Magento and add your own pieces of code to it. In certain situations they are slightly underestimated by extension developers, either due to their knowledge of the platform, or due to the lack of grand vision or forced quick and dirty implementations.

Events and observers are the key to writing unobtrusive code in cases where you need to change or add to the default Magento behavior. For example, if you need to send all your newly created orders to an external fulfillment system, most of the time you simply need to observe a proper event and implement your business logic within an observer.

There are several types of events getting fired in Magento depending on how you differentiate them. For example, we could divide them into static and dynamic events.

Static events are all those events defined through code with full event names such as `Mage::dispatchEvent('admin_session_user_login_failed', array('user_name' => $username, 'exception' => $e));`, `Mage::dispatchEvent('cms_page_prepare_save', array('page' => $model, 'request' => $this->getRequest()));`, `Mage::dispatchEvent('catalog_product_get_final_price', array('product' => $product, 'qty' => $qty));`, `Mage::dispatchEvent('catalog_product_flat_prepare_columns', array('columns' => $columnsObject));`, and `Mage::dispatchEvent('catalog_prepare_price_select', $eventArgs);`.

Dynamic events are all those events defined through code dynamically at runtime such as `Mage::dispatchEvent($this->_eventPrefix.'_load_before', $params);`, `Mage::dispatchEvent($this->_eventPrefix.'_load_after', $this->_getEventData());`, `Mage::dispatchEvent($this->_eventPrefix.'_save_before', $this->_getEventData());`, `Mage::dispatchEvent($this->_eventPrefix.'_save_after', $this->_getEventData());`, and `Mage::dispatchEvent('controller_action_layout_render_before_'.$this->getFullActionName());`.

Both types of events are absolutely the same; they function the same, and the preceding differentiation is simply a matter of terminology. We are calling the other ones dynamic because their full name is not known until the runtime.

For example, each time you wish to intercept certain parameters passed to a controller action, you could simply create an event observer that would observe the `controller_action_predispatch_*` event, which is triggered within the `Mage_Core_Controller_Varien_Action` class file as follows: `Mage::dispatchEvent('controller_action_predispatch_' . $this->getFullActionName(), array('controller_action' => $this));`.

Now, let us see how exactly do we define the event observer and place some of our code to be executed upon certain events. First, we need to create an entry within our extensions `config.xml` file.

Let's say we want to introspect all the parameters passed to the controller action during the customer registration process. When a customer fills in the required registration fields and clicks on Submit, the form posts the data to the `http://{{shop.domain}}/index.php/customer/account/createpost/` URL.

If you look at the previously mentioned the `controller_action_predispatch_*` event, the expression `$this->getFullActionName()` would return the `customer_account_createpost string`. You can find that out easily by placing the `var_dump($this->getFullActionName()); exit;` expression right there under the `Mage::dispatchEvent('controller_action_predispatch_...` expression. Please note that we are using `var_dump` here just for the simplicity of demonstration. So now that we know this, we can safely conclude that the full event name we need to observe in this case is `controller_action_predispatch_customer_account_createpost`.

Now we know that the event name is a requirement upon which we create a proper `config.xml` entry for defining our event observer as shown in the following code:

```
<?xml version="1.0"?>
<config>
   <!-- … other elements ... -->
   <frontend>
      <events>
         <controller_action_predispatch_customer_account_createpost>
            <observers>
              <foggyline_happyhour_intercept>
                 <class>foggyline_happyhour/observerobserver</class>
                 <method>intercept</method>
                 </foggyline_happyhour_intercept>
              </observers>
         </controller_action_predispatch_customer_account_createpost>
      </events>
   </frontend>
   <!-- … other elements ... -->
</config>
```

Within the observer's element comes the definition of our observer, which we call `foggyline_happyhour_intercept` in this case. Each observer needs two properties-defined classes, which in this case points to the `foggyline_happyhour` class group and `Observer` class file thus, the string `foggyline_happyhour/observer`; the other one is the method within the `Observer` class file.

Next, we create the actual `Observer` class file `app/code/community/Foggyline/HappyHour/Model/Observer.php` with the following content:

```
<?php

class Foggyline_HappyHour_Model_Observer
{
    public function intercept($observer = null)
    {
        $event = $observer->getEvent();
        $controllerAction = $event->getControllerAction();
        $params = $controllerAction->getRequest()->getParams();

        Mage::log($params);
    }
}
```

A quick look at `Foggyline_HappyHour_Model_Observer` reveals one important thing: unlike `Model`, `Block`, and `Controller` classes, the `Observer` classes do not need to extend anything.

If you now go to your browser and try to create a new customer account, you will get your `var/log/system.log` file filled with the HTTP POST parameters provided by the customer during the registration process. You might need to refresh/re-open `system.log` in your editor in order to pick up the changes, in case you don't see the log entries.

Sometimes, the right event might not be there; so you might need to look for the second best. For example, if we did not have the `controller_action_predispatch_customer_account_createpost` event dispatched, the next best event would probably be the following one: `Mage::dispatchEvent('controller_action_predispatch', array('controller_action' => $this));`.

However, the event `controller_action_predispatch` is pretty generic, which means it will get triggered for every controller action `predispatch`. In this case, you would have to do a little if/else logic within your event observer code. Just as we have controller fired events, we also have model-fired events. If you open a class file like `Mage_Catalog_Model_Product`, you can see property definitions like `protected $_eventPrefix = 'catalog_product';` and `protected $_eventObject = 'product';`.

Now, if you trace the code a little bit down to the `Mage_Core_Model_Abstract` class file, you will see that the properties `$_eventPrefix` and `$_eventObject` are used for dynamic events such as (along with the static events for the same action) `Mage::dispatchEvent($this->_eventPrefix.'_load_before', $params);`, `Mage::dispatchEvent($this->_eventPrefix.'_load_after', $this->_getEventData());`, `Mage::dispatchEvent($this->_eventPrefix.'_save_commit_after', $this->_getEventData());`, `Mage::dispatchEvent($this->_eventPrefix.'_save_before', $this->_getEventData());`, `Mage::dispatchEvent($this->_eventPrefix.'_save_after', $this->_getEventData());`, `Mage::dispatchEvent($this->_eventPrefix.'_delete_before', $this->_getEventData());`, `Mage::dispatchEvent($this->_eventPrefix.'_delete_after', $this->_getEventData());`, `Mage::dispatchEvent($this->_eventPrefix.'_delete_commit_after', $this->_getEventData());`, and `Mage::dispatchEvent($this->_eventPrefix.'_clear', $this->_getEventData());`.

Knowing this is extremely important, as it enables you to create all sorts of event observers for specific models and their actions, for example customer, order, and invoice entity create/update/delete actions. This is why defining the `$_eventPrefix` and `$_eventObject` properties on your custom model classes is something you should adopt as a sign of good coding practice. Doing so enables other third-party developers to easily hook onto your extension code via the observer in a clean and unobtrusive way.

Cron jobs

Cron jobs are used to schedule commands to be executed periodically by the cron. Cron is a a time-based job scheduler software in Unix-like computer operating systems. It is driven by a `crontab` (cron table) file, a configuration file that specifies shell commands to run periodically on a given schedule.

Magento cron jobs is a different kind of functionality than that just mentioned. It merely relies on the system cron software to trigger the root Magento `cron.php` or `cron.sh` files periodically. Keep that in mind while talking about cron and Magento cron jobs.

It is highly important that the system administrator has the system cron set to trigger the Magento `cron.sh` file at regular intervals, at least every five minutes. This can be done by adding the following line to system cron:`*/5 * * * * /path/to /magento/root/folder/cron.sh`. This way, you as a Magento extension developer have the ability to create a new Magento cron jobs definitions through your extensions configuration files and rest assured they will get executed. Magento cron jobs are defined in the `config.xml` file as follows:

```
<?xml version="1.0"?>
<config>
<!-- … other elements ... -->
    <crontab>
        <jobs>
            <foggyline_happyhour_ordersToFulfilment>
                <schedule>
                    <cron_expr>*/2 * * * *</cron_expr>
                </schedule>
                <run>
                    <model>foggyline_happyhour/
service::ordersToFulfilment</model>
                </run>
            </foggyline_happyhour_ordersToFulfilment>
        </jobs>
    </crontab>
<!-- … other elements ... -->
</config>
```

In this example, our cron job has been defined with the name `foggyline_happyhour_ordersToFulfilment` and set to execute every two minutes, which can be seen by the `schedule >cron_expr` value. For more details on writing cron expressions, check out the following URL: `http://en.wikipedia.org/wiki/Cron`.

The `model` element, which in this case is set to `foggyline_happyhour/service::ordersToFulfilment`, means that the following code from the `app/code/community/Foggyline/HappyHour/Model/Service.php` file would get executed by this cron job:

```
<?php

class Foggyline_HappyHour_Model_Service
{
    public function ping()
    {
        Mage::log('ping');
    }
}
```

The same as with observer classes, cron-defined model classes do not need to extend anything.

Even though this Magento cron job has been set to run every two minutes, you as an extension developer have no guarantee that the system cron will ever be run on a third-party website, or if it's run it might not be run in small enough intervals. Thus, you might end up with a code logic that never gets executed, or gets executed in larger than planned intervals.

During development, however, you do not need to have the system cron set up. It is sufficient to just execute the `http://magento.loc/cron.php` URL in the browser, as this will trigger the Magento cron system.

For example, if you were writing an extension that has one or more Magento cron jobs defined in `config.xml`, the easiest way to check if you correctly defined your cron job would be to truncate the `cron_schedule` database table and then trigger the `http://magento.loc/cron.php` URL in the browser. Obviously, in this case, later on you would have to periodically trigger the `http://magento.loc/cron.php` URL to check if your cron job execution went through, monitoring the `executed_at` column within the `cron_schedule` database table.

Helpers

There is one part of Magento functionality that gets equally used across all the individual functionality mentioned so far, and that's **helpers**. Magento helper is a class that usually extends the `Mage_Core_Helper_Data` class directly found in the `app/code/core/Mage/Core/Helper/Data.php` file or at the very least derived from the `Mage_Core_Helper_Abstract` class found under the `app/code/core/Mage/Core/Helper/Abstract.php` file.

The `Helper` classes contain various utility methods that will allow you to perform common tasks on different objects and variables. Helpers too are defined via the `config.xml` elements as follows:

```
<?xml version="1.0"?>
<config>
   <!-- … other elements ... -->
   <global>
      <helpers>
         <foggyline_happyhour>
            <class>Foggyline_HappyHour_Helper</class>
         </foggyline_happyhour>
      </helpers>
   </global>
   <!-- … other elements ... -->
</config>
```

Similar to blocks and models, helpers have a class element defined to point to their folder locations within an extension. In this example, a helper is defined with the name `foggyline_happyhour`.

As you are allowed to have multiple helpers under the `app/code/community/Foggyline/HappyHour/Helper/` folder, it is important to know that the default helper PHP filename is `Data.php`.

What this really means is that when you execute a statement such as `Mage::helper('foggyline_happyhour');`, Magento will load the `Data.php` helper. If, however, you execute a statement such as `Mage::helper('foggyline_happyhour/image');`, Magento will load the `Image.php` helper (the `app/code/community/Foggyline/HappyHour/Helper/Image.php` file).

System configuration options

Besides being a utility method container, the `Helper` classes play an indispensable role for extensions that provide Magento-style configuration options for users. For example, if you were building a payment extension, you would most certainly need a configuration area in order to set up the access data for it. Magento comes with its own built-in configuration area, located under **System** | **Configuration**. This entire section is built from the XML elements found under the extension `etc/system.xml`.

Here is where things get a little complicated. In order for the Magento admin user to have access to your extension configuration interface defined through `system.xml`, it needs permissions for that. These permissions are defined in another configuration file located in the same folder called `adminhtml.xml`.

Let us demonstrate this with a simple example. We will create a configuration options section for our extension within `system.xml`, define permissions to it via `adminhtml.xml`, and then use the data helper class to fetch that configuration value from within our controller.

First, we need to create the `app/code/community/Foggyline/HappyHour/etc/system.xml` configuration file with the following content:

```
<?xml version="1.0"?>
<config>
   <tabs>
      <foggyline module="foggyline_happyhour">">
         <label>Foggyline</label>
        <sort_order>10</sort_order>
      </foggyline>
   </tabs>
```

```
        <sections>
            <foggyline_happyhour module="foggyline_happyhour">
                <label>FoggylineHappyHour</label>
                <tab>foggyline</tab>
                <sort_order>10</sort_order>
                <show_in_default>1</show_in_default>
                <groups>
                    <settings>
                        <label>FoggylineHappyHour Settings</label>
                        <sort_order>10</sort_order>
                        <show_in_default>1</show_in_default>
                        <fields>
                            <custom_message>
                                <label>Custom Message</label>
                                <frontend_type>text</frontend_type>
                                <sort_order>20</sort_order>
                                <show_in_default>1</show_in_default>
                            </custom_message>
                        </fields>
                    </settings>
                </groups>
            </foggyline_happyhour>
        </sections>
    </config>
```

The first thing that we did was add a custom tab called **Foggyline** to the system configuration. Tabs are the navigation headers down the left-hand side of the Magento administration are a under **System | Configuration**. The default tabs are **General**, **Catalog**, **Customers**, **Sales**, **Services**, and **Advanced**. Adding a new tab is as simple as defining your own element under **Configuration | Tabs**. In our example, we have defined the `foggyline` element, where `foggyline` is a freely given element name. The attribute `module="foggyline_happyhour"` simply tells Magento what helper to use for this part of functionality while referencing helpers internally. The string `foggyline_happyhour` points to the helper group defined under `config.xml`. The `label` element specifies the label for this tab to be shown under the navigation sidebar. The `sort_order` element specifies the order in the sidebar with regards to other elements; a larger number pushes the item in the sidebar to the bottom after other elements.

Once we have defined the actual tab, we need to add one or more sections to it. In our example, we have defined one section through the `foggyline_happyhour` element.

The `foggyline_happyhour` element is an arbitrary name that's used to identify your new section.

The `label` element defines the display value used in the HTML interface for your new section.

The `tab` element identifies which tab your new section should be grouped under. We want our section to show up under our new **Foggyline** tab. The name foggyline comes from the tag used to create the **Foggyline** tab.

The `sort_order` element determines where this section shows up vertically compared to other sections in the tab.

The `show_in_default` element is a Boolean configuration option with a valid value of 1 or 0. They determine the level of configuration scope this section has.

The `groups` element determines the logical grouping of configuration options, sort of like the `fieldset` element in HTML forms.

The `settings` element within groups is an arbitrary name that's used to identify this group.

The elements `label`, `sort_order`, and `show_in_default` are analogous to those previously explained for this section.

The `fields` element is a container for one or more elements that will be visually manifested into HTML form elements later. Within the `fields` element, again we have `label`, `sort_order`, `show_in_default`, and this time one new element called `frontend_type`. The `frontend_type` element determines what HTML element will be used for rendering in the browser.

At this point if you try to log in to Magento and navigate to **System** | **Configuration**, you will be able to see the **FoggylineHappyHour** menu in the left sidebar. However, accessing the menu item would give you a **404 Error Page not found** error.

This might be a good time to explain what ACL actually is. **ACL**, short for **Access Control Lists**, is a functionality that allows a store owner to create fine-grained roles for each and every user in their system. A default Magento installation comes with one role, Administrators. Magento ACL implementation allows you to add new roles to the system via **System** | **Permissions** | **Roles**. A role is essentially a collection of resources, while a resource is basically an action such as "delete user".

While adding new system configuration sections, you need to define resources for it so that Magento can use it via its ACL system. So the reason why we might be getting a **404 Error Page not found** error is that we are missing the ACL definition.

This is why we need to create the `app/code/community/Foggyline/HappyHour/etc/adminhtml.xml` file with the following content:

```
<?xml version="1.0"?>
<config>
   <acl>
      <resources>
         <admin>
            <children>
               <system>
                  <children>
                     <config>
                        <children>
                           <foggyline_happyhour module="foggyline_
happyhour">">
                              <title>FoggylineHappyHour</title>
                           </foggyline_happyhour>
                        </children>
                     </config>
                  </children>
               </system>
            </children>
         </admin>
      </resources>
   </acl>
</config>
```

Once done, you need to log out and then log back in to Magento administration in order for `acl` (access list) to kick in, otherwise you will still be getting a **404 Error Page not found** error when you try to access **System** | **Configuration** | **Foggyline** | **FoggylineHappyHour**.

Now get back to the `adminhtml.xml` file. The syntax of the file seems somewhat recursive with all those children elements repeating. We could say that we need to define a resource whose path matches the system configuration option defined under `system.xml`. So if a base path for the `acl` resource within `adminhtml.xml` is `config > acl > resources > admin > children > system > children > config > children`, we simply need to define a new child within it called `foggyline_happyhour` like we did in the preceding example. The element name `foggyline_happyhour` must match the element name of the section from within `system.xml`.

The `title` element simply dictates what will show up in the Magento administration panel when the node tree is displayed.

If all went well, you should be able to see your configuration options interface as shown in the following screenshot:

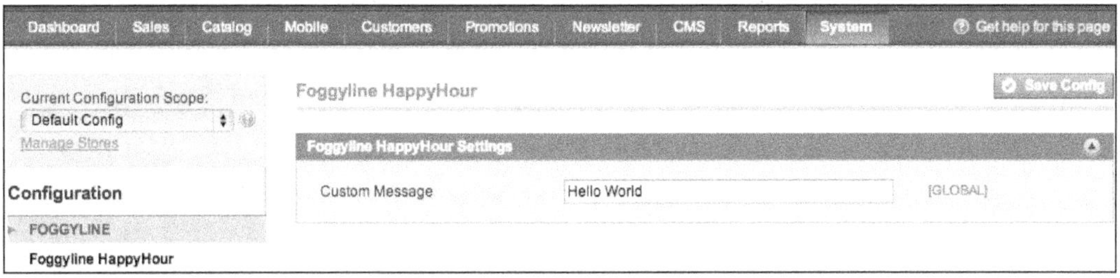

Magento allows each configuration option defined through `system.xml` to have a default value. For example, let's say we want the default value of our `custom_message` to be Hello World string. To do so, we turn to our `config.xml` file as follows:

```
<?xml version="1.0"?>
<config>
   <!-- … other elements ... -->
   <default>
      <foggyline_happyhour>
         <settings>
            <custom_message><![CDATA[Hello World]]></custom_message>
         </settings>
      </foggyline_happyhour>
   </default>
   <!-- … other elements ... -->
</config>
```

It might look a bit confusing at first, but notice how the `config.xml` element paths within the default element path `foggyline_happyhour> settings >foggyline_happyhour` follow the `system.xml` element paths within the sections element path `foggyline_happyhour> settings > foggyline_happyhour` (minus the `groups` element). Now if you open the **System** | **Configuration** | **Foggyline** | **FoggylineHappyHour**, you should see, if you haven't previously saved some other value, the text `Hello World` under the **Custom Message** option value.

Finally, as shown in the following code snippet, we will use the helper `Data` class to add utility methods for extracting our configuration option value from the `system.xml`:

```
<?php

class Foggyline_HappyHour_Helper_Data extends Mage_Core_Helper_Data
{
   const XML_PATH_CUSTOM_MESSAGE = 'foggyline_happyhour/settings/
custom_message';

   public function getCustomMessage($storestore = null)
   {
      return Mage::getStoreConfig(self::XML_PATH_CUSTOM_MESSAGE,
$store);
   }
}
```

Looking at the preceding code, it is easy to conclude how the `const XML_PATH_CUSTOM_MESSAGE` string value follows the same XML elements path as previously mentioned for `system.xml` and `config.xml`. Passing that string to `Mage::getStoreConfig()` will retrieve our custom message.

To confirm everything is working, add the following action to your `app/code/community/Foggyline/HappyHour/controllers/HelloController.php` class file:

```
<?php

class Foggyline_HappyHour_HelloController extends Mage_Core_
Controller_Front_Action
{
   public function helperTestAction()
   {
      echo Mage::helper('foggyline_happyhour')->getCustomMessage();
   }
}
```

Now open the `http://magento.loc/index.php/happyhour/hello/helperTest` URL in the browser; if all is good, you should be able to see the Hello World message.

Even though we have covered a lot of ground so far, we have barely scratched the surface. The massiveness of the Magento platform hides far more features. These, however, are left for you to discover.

Magento is known for its poor developer documentation regarding certain features. Every now and then you will find yourself tracing the Magento core code trying to understand its inner workings. Hopefully, the preceding introduction will give you a good starting point.

Summary

Up until now, we have covered the basics of Magento's overall structure. We took a dive into the extension structure itself. As we progressed through individual extension structures, we familiarized ourselves with configuration file, Model, Block, Helper, controller classes, and a few other important concepts. We gave a brief intro to the Magento event/observer pattern, cron jobs functionality, and access lists. With this combined knowledge, we should now be ready for the next chapter, the full-blown extension.

2

Building the Extension – Maximum Order Amount

If you successfully made it through the first chapter, it is time to use what we have learned so far and get our hands dirty with building a real and usable extension. The functional requirement of the extension that we are going to develop is a simple, light fraud-prevention mechanism. The merchant needs a configuration option through which he can set a maximum order amount allowed for purchase and an e-mail notification for orders above certain suspicious amount. Functionality like this can serve as a mini fraud-protection system.

Planning your extension

Once you are clear with the basic functional requirement, you should take some time to think about its implementation in the form of a Magento extension. For example, an extension like this would require the following contents:

- A `system.xml` file through which we would define configuration options, one of which is the maximum allowed order amount
- Usage of a proper event observer through which we would observe products being added to the cart, and then intercept the addition of entirely new products or product quantities that would break the maximum order amount barrier when added to the cart

Registering your extension

The following is a list of steps required for successfully registering your extension via configuration files:

1. We start off by defining our extension namespace, which is usually our company name or website domain, or something else that is unique to us. In our case, the namespace will be `Foggyline`. Once we define the namespace, we need to define our extension name; let's call it `MaxOrderAmount`.
2. Next, we need to decide on `codePool`. Since we will distribute this extension to more than one merchant, possibly uploading it to Magento Connect, the decision is simple; we will use `community` as `codePool`.
3. Now we go ahead and create an extension registration file, `app/etc/modules/Foggyline_MaxOrderAmount.xml`, with the following code content:

```
<?xml version="1.0" encoding="UTF-8"?>
<config>
  <modules>
    <Foggyline_MaxOrderAmount>
      <active>true</active>
      <codePool>community</codePool>
    </Foggyline_MaxOrderAmount>
  </modules>
</config>
```

4. Once the file is in place, log in to the Magento administration interface, then navigate to **System** | **Configuration** | **Advanced** | **Advanced**. You should see your extension appear on the Disable Module Output list.

> If for some reason you do not see your extension there on the list, then navigate to **System** | **Cache** and click on the **Clear Magento Cache** button. If you still do not see your extension on the Disable Module Output list, then the chances are that you have an invalid XML within the `Foggyline_MaxOrderAmount.xml` file or possible file access permission restrictions.

5. Once you confirm that Magento sees your extension, the next file we need to create is `app/code/community/Foggyline/MaxOrderAmount/etc/config.xml` with the following initial code content:

```
<?xml version="1.0" encoding="UTF-8"?>
<config>
  <modules>
    <Foggyline_MaxOrderAmount>
```

```
        <version>1.0.0.0</version>
      </Foggyline_MaxOrderAmount>
    </modules>
  </global>
</config>
```

> This is the so-called extension configuration file, in which we define models, helpers, blocks, routers, and many other things.

Building the configuration options interface

The following is a list of steps for defining the system configuration options for your extension:

1. We will first go ahead and build our configuration option's interface. Thus we need to create the `app/code/community/Foggyline/MaxOrderAmount/etc/system.xml` file with the following code content:

```
<?xml version="1.0" encoding="UTF-8"?>
<config>
  <sections>
    <sales module="sales">
      <groups>
        <foggyline_maxorderamount>
          <label>Maximum Order Amount</label>
          <sort_order>10</sort_order>
          <show_in_default>1</show_in_default>
          <show_in_website>1</show_in_website>
          <show_in_store>1</show_in_store>
          <fields>
            <active>
              <label>Enable</label>
              <sort_order>10</sort_order>
              <frontend_type>select</frontend_type>
              <source_model>
                adminhtml/system_config_source_yesno
                  </source_model>
              <show_in_default>
                1</show_in_default>
              <show_in_website>
                1</show_in_website>
```

```
              <show_in_store>
                0</show_in_store>
            </active>
            <single_order_top_amount>
              <label>Single Order Maximum Amount</label>
              <frontend_type>text</frontend_type>
              <sort_order>20</sort_order>
              <show_in_default>1</show_in_default>
              <show_in_website>1</show_in_website>
              <show_in_store>0</show_in_store>
            </single_order_top_amount>
            <single_order_top_amount_msg>
              <label>Single Order Maximum Amount
                Message</label>
              <frontend_type>text</frontend_type>
              <sort_order>30</sort_order>
              <show_in_default>1</show_in_default>
              <show_in_website>1</show_in_website>
              <show_in_store>0</show_in_store>
            </single_order_top_amount_msg>
          </fields>
        </foggyline_maxorderamount>
      </groups>
    </sales>
  </sections>
</config>
```

This is quite a big chunk of XML code, but do not be afraid, since we should already be familiar with its structure from the first chapter. There are a few new XML elements here; however, if you take a look under the individual field's element definition, for example `single_order_top_amount`, you can see elements, namely `show_in_default`, `show_in_website`, `show_in_store`. Since Magento is a multiwebsite or multistore platform, these are used internally to enable you to set and get configuration options all the way down to individual store level. For example, our configuration options won't be visible on the backend when the admin changes the configuration scope to store level, since `show_in_store` is set to `0`.

The `source_model` element is used to supply possible options through a model class that you specify. The value we supply here is in the `form model class group /` directory, and the file path `Directory Mage/Adminhtml/Model/System/Config/Source` contains a lot of useful sources already defined, such as Yes or No, or Enable or Disable, or lists of countries, currencies, or languages. In our example, we are basically using a `Mage/Adminhtml/Model/System/Config/Source/Yesno.php` class file.

Depending on what type of extensions you are developing, you might never need to use `show_in_store`, or even `show_in_website`. In *Chapter 1, An Overview of Magento Extensions*, the `system.xml` file had a definition of the `tab` element. Here, we are not creating our own tab, thus we do not need to define it. The element `config/sections/sales` has already been defined under Magento core extension, called `Mage_Sales`, so on defining it again here Magento sees as simply extending it. This is why we have defined the `groups` element only, with our specific `foggyline_maxorderamount` element under it, in order to prevent rewriting the entire `sales` element.

2. Once we have `system.xml` all in place, we need to log in to Magento and navigate to **System** | **Configuration** | **Sales** to confirm that Magento sees it. You should see your configuration options here.

   If all is OK, we get back to our config.xml. There we will add default values to some of our configuration options defined under `system.xml` as shown in the following code:

```
<?xml version="1.0" encoding="UTF-8"?>
<config>
  <!-- ...other elements... -->
  <default>
    <sales>
      <foggyline_maxorderamount>
        <active>0</active>
        <single_order_top_amount>
          15001500</single_order_top_amount>
        <single_order_top_amount_msg>
          <![CDATA[No single order allowed with amount over
            %s.]]></single_order_top_amount_msg>
      </foggyline_maxorderamount>
    </sales>
  </default>
  <!-- ...other elements... -->
</config>
```

> Our next move will be to write a helper that will read these configuration values. However, before we write the helper, we need to define its class group under `config.xml`. While there we will add class group definitions for models as well.

3. Edit the `config.xml` file by adding the following to it:

```
<?xml version="1.0" encoding="UTF-8"?>
<config>
  <!-- ...other elements... -->
  <global>
    <models>
      <foggyline_maxorderamount>
        <class>Foggyline_MaxOrderAmount_Model</class>
      </foggyline_maxorderamount>
    </models>
    <helpers>
      <foggyline_maxorderamount>
        <class>Foggyline_MaxOrderAmount_Helper</class>
      </foggyline_maxorderamount>
    </helpers>
  </global>
  <!-- ...other elements... -->
</config>
```

4. Now, we can go ahead and create our `app/code/community/Foggyline/MaxOrderAmount/Helper/Data.php` file with the following code content:

```
<?php
class Foggyline_MaxOrderAmount_Helper_Data extends
  Mage_Core_Helper_Abstract
{
  const XML_PATH_ACTIVE =
    'sales/foggyline_maxorderamount/active';
  const XML_PATH_SINGLE_ORDER_TOP_AMOUNT =
    'sales/foggyline_maxorderamount/
      single_order_top_amount';
  const XML_PATH_SINGLE_ORDER_TOP_AMOUNT_MSG =
    'sales/foggyline_maxorderamount/
      single_order_top_amount_msg';

  public function isModuleEnabled($moduleName = null)
  {
    if ((int)Mage::getStoreConfig(self::XML_PATH_ACTIVE,
      Mage::app()->getStore()) != 1) {
      return false;
    }
    return parent::isModuleEnabled($moduleName );
  }
```

```
    public function getSingleOrderTopAmount($store = null)
    {
      return
        (int)Mage::getStoreConfig
          (self::XML_PATH_SINGLE_ORDER_TOP_AMOUNT, $store);
    }

    public function getSingleOrderTopAmountMsg($store = null)
    {
      return
        Mage::getStoreConfig
          (self::XML_PATH_SINGLE_ORDER_TOP_AMOUNT_MSG,
            $store);
    }
  }
```

The helper class is pretty straightforward and simple. In this extension, it will serve merely to read configuration values. The most important thing here, and one that causes most errors if not done right, is the value of all those `XML_PATH_*` constants. These values must follow the same `config.xml` and `system.xml` element tree, for example `sales/foggyline_maxorderamount/single_order_top_amount` from within `Data.php` must follow the `sections/sales/groups/foggyline_maxorderamount/fields/single_order_top_amount` element's structure from within `system.xml` (minus the sections, groups, and fields as these are stripped by the internal Magento system).

Adding the business logic

Now that we have registered our extension with Magento and defined the required configuration options, it's time to add the business logic as described in the following steps:

1. Add the event observer to our config.xml file as shown in the following code:

```
<?xml version="1.0" encoding="UTF-8"?>
<config>
  <!-- ...other elements... -->
    <frontend>
      <events>
        <sales_quote_save_before>
          <observers>
            <foggyline_maxorderamount_
              enforceSingleOrderLimit>
```

```
                <class>
                  foggyline_maxorderamount/observer</class>
                  <method>enforceSingleOrderLimit</method>
              </foggyline_maxorderamount_
                enforceSingleOrderLimit>
            </observers>
          </sales_quote_save_before>
        </events>
      </frontend>
    <!-- ...other elements... -->
  </config>
```

Event observers can be placed under `config/global`, `config/adminhtml`, and `config/frontend`. Our extension uses `config/frontend` because in Magento, the same event can be fired on the frontend and on the administration area, for example `Product` entity after the `save` event. Sometimes, depending on your extension functionality, you might want to observe only events fired from either the frontend or administration area. In our extension, we do not want to put the maximum order amount restriction on the administration, thus blocking the admin users from creating large orders, so we placed our event observer under `config/frontend`. The reason why we choose exactly the `sales_quote_save_before` event to observe is a bit more difficult to explain. This is one of those dynamic events we described under *Chapter 1, An Overview of Magento Extensions*. When a customer adds a product to the cart, Magento internally modifies its singleton instance of the `Mage_Sales_Model_Quote` object. This object further contains a collection of the `Mage_Sales_Model_Quote_Item` objects. For every product you add to the cart, Magento creates an instance of `Mage_Sales_Model_Quote_Item`, which it then further persists into a database. The `sales_quote_save_before` event is especially interesting to us in this case, because if an error occurs during its execution, Magento will fail to save the object, and its possibly newly updated item's collection. What this means is that with an error within the observer, products won't be added to the cart. This fits perfectly for our extension functionality as it will enable us to achieve the desired effect with just a few lines of code.

2. Now that we understand the reason for choosing the `sales_quote_save_before` event, go ahead and create the `app/code/community/Foggyline/MaxOrderAmount/Model/Observer.php` file with the following code content:

```
<?php

class Foggyline_MaxOrderAmount_Model_Observer
{
```

```
    public function enforceSingleOrderLimit($observer)
    {
      $helper = Mage::helper('foggyline_maxorderamount');
      if (!$helper->isModuleEnabled()) {
        return;
      }

      $quote = $observer->getEvent()->getQuote();

      if ((float)$quote->getGrandTotal() >
        (float)$helper->getSingleOrderTopAmount()) {

        $formattedPrice =
          Mage::helper('core')->currency($helper-
            >getSingleOrderTopAmount(), true, false);

        Mage::getSingleton('checkout/session')->addError(
        $helper->__($helper->getSingleOrderTopAmountMsg(),
          $formattedPrice));

        Mage::app()->getFrontController()->getResponse()-
          >setRedirect(Mage::getUrl('checkout/cart'));
        Mage::app()->getResponse()->sendResponse();
        exit;
      }
    }
  }
```

Code within the `enforceSingleOrderLimit()` method is pretty self-explanatory. First, we are grabbing the `quote` object from the event. There is no magic here, just remember the dynamic events, in this case, originating from the `Mage_Core_Model_Abstract` method. Once we have the `quote` object instance, we can compare its grand total value with the value set for the maximum order amount. If the grand total value is greater than the maximum order amount allowed, then we add the error message to the checkout session and redirect the user to the cart page.

Now that everything is in place, you can go ahead and test your functionality. If you haven't changed the default values for the `single_order_top_amount` configuration option, then adding the product to the cart with the total price over $1500 (or other currently active currency) will trigger the **No single order allowed with amount over %s.** message.

This extension is an example of a relatively simple Magento extension that requires a bit more advanced and experience-based knowledge of the Magento order quote system.

Summary

In this chapter, we learned how to create an extension from scratch. Specific to this extension was the usage of an event or observer pattern. We got in touch with the system configuration section by defining our own configuration option. Values assigned to this configuration option were then read via the help of a Helper class that we defined. In *Chapter 3, Building the Extension - Logger*, we will build a new extension, expanding our knowledge with installation scripts, models, and the other building blocks of an extension.

3
Building the Extension – Logger

Moving forward with deepening our knowledge of Magento extensions, we will familiarize ourselves with models, blocks, controllers, and other things throughout this chapter. Unlike the Maximum Order Amount extension that we wrote in *Chapter 1, An Overview of Magento Extensions*, that affected the customer part of functionality, the **Logger** extension will be geared toward admin users. The functional requirement of an extension is simple and it improves the logging system so that the admin user gets an interface through which he can see all standard Magento logs recorded using the `Mage::log()` method. The default Magento logging system only stores text entries under `/var/system.log`, `/var/exception.log`, or other custom logfiles.

Planning your extension

Once you are clear with the basic functional requirement, you should take some time to think about its implementation in the form of Magento extension, just as we did in a previous chapter. For example, a similar extension would require the following files:

- The `adminhtml.xml` file through which we will define admin menu for accessing the logger grid listing
- The `config.xml` file through which we will define our Logger model, admin router for listing our logger block entities
- Various blocks, models, and controller class files

Registering your extension

The following are the steps to register your extension:

1. Governed by the same rules from *Chapter 2, Building the Extension - Maximum Order Amount*, we will first set a name and location for our extension. Our extension will be named as `Foggyline_Logger` and will be located under `community codePool`.
2. Now, we need to create an extension of the registration file `app/etc/modules/Foggyline_Logger.xml` with the following code content:

```
<?xml version="1.0"?>
<config>
  <modules>
    <Foggyline_Logger>
      <active>true</active>
      <codePool>community</codePool>
      <depends>
        <Mage_Core/>
      </depends>
    </Foggyline_Logger>
  </modules>
</config>
```

3. Once the file is in place, you need to confirm that Magento can see it under **System** | **Configuration** | **Advanced** | **Advanced**. You will see your extension appear on the Disable Module Output list.
4. Once you confirm that Magento sees your extension, the next file we need to create is `app/code/community/Foggyline/Logger/etc/config.xml` with the following initial code content:

```
<?xml version="1.0" encoding="UTF-8"?>
<config>
  <modules>
    <Foggyline_Logger>
      <version>1.0.0.0</version>
    </Foggyline_Logger>
  </modules>
</config>
```

> Remember, this is the so-called `extension configuration` file.

Setting up the model and install script

Since the basis of our extension functionality is to intercept the default `Mage::log()` method calls and write the log entries to the database, we need to set up the model and install a script that would create the necessary table for our model entity, by performing the following steps:

1. Go ahead and add the following XML entities to your `config.xml` file.

```
<?xml version="1.0" encoding="UTF-8"?>
<config>
<!-- ...other elements... -->
  <global>
    <models>
      <foggyline_logger>
        <class>Foggyline_Logger_Model</class>
        <resourceModel>
          foggyline_logger_resource</resourceModel>
      </foggyline_logger>
      <foggyline_logger_resource>
        <class>Foggyline_Logger_Model_Resource</class>
        <entities>
          <logger>
            <table>foggyline_logger_logger</table>
          </logger>
        </entities>
      </foggyline_logger_resource>
    </models>
    <resources>
      <foggyline_logger_setup>
        <setup>
          <module>Foggyline_Logger</module>
        </setup>
      </foggyline_logger_setup>
    </resources>
    <helpers>
      <foggyline_logger>
        <class>Foggyline_Logger_Helper</class>
      </foggyline_logger>
    </helpers>
  </global>
<!-- ...other elements... -->
</config>
```

Several things are happening in the previous code. Remember how we said in *Chapter 1, An Overview of Magento Extensions*, that each entity model which is to be persisted in a database needs to have four files defined. XML element definitions that we just added in the previous code match the locations of those four files. The `config/global/models/foggyline_logger/class` path matches the part of the directory path where our model files will be stored. Within this XML path definition, the `foggyline_logger` element is named in a free manner, usually matching our extension name. The `config/global/models/foggyline_logger/resourceModel` path stores a value that points to the `config/global/models/foggyline_logger_resource` path, where we define our `model resource` folder through the `class` element definition and any entity model that will have a table in the database through the entities element definition. The `foggyline_logger_resource` element is given a free name, usually matching the "our extension name" and `_resource` formula. The same goes for the `foggyline_logger_resource/entities/logger` element, where the logger is freely given an XML element name. Within the logger element, we have the `table` element definition, whose value is set to `foggyline_logger_logger`, which is what our database table will be called. If you are new to Magento, there is a lot to digest here. Usually, developers who are new to Magento have this "XML is easy, as long as I know where these element names come from" reaction.

Finally, the XML path `config/global/resources/foggyline_logger_setup` is used for setting the installation script folder location within our extension's SQL directory.

2. Let's go ahead and create an installation `app/code/community/Foggyline/Logger/sql/ foggyline_logger_setup/install-1.0.0.0.php` file with the following code content:

```
<?php

$installer = $this;

$installer->startSetup();

$table = $installer->getConnection()
  ->newTable($installer-
    >getTable('foggyline_logger/logger'))
  ->addColumn('entity_id',
    Varien_Db_Ddl_Table::TYPE_INTEGER, null, array(
    'identity'  => true,
    'unsigned'  => true,
    'nullable'  => false,
```

```
        'primary'    => true,
    ), 'Id')
    ->addColumn('timestamp', Varien_Db_Ddl_Table::TYPE_CHAR,
      25, array(
        'nullable'  => false,
    ), 'Timestamp')
    ->addColumn('message', Varien_Db_Ddl_Table::TYPE_TEXT,
      null, array(
        'nullable'  => false,
    ), 'Message')
    ->addColumn('priority',
      Varien_Db_Ddl_Table::TYPE_INTEGER, 2, array(
        'nullable'  => false,
    ), 'Priority')
    ->addColumn('priority_name',
      Varien_Db_Ddl_Table::TYPE_VARCHAR, 32, array(
        'nullable'  => false,
    ), 'Priority Name')
    ->addColumn('file', Varien_Db_Ddl_Table::TYPE_TEXT, null,
      array(
        'nullable'  => false,
    ), 'File');
$installer->getConnection()->createTable($table);

$installer->endSetup();
```

> For more insight into the inner workings of `$this ($installer)` object, take some time to study the code within the following two classes:
>
> `Mage_Core_Model_Resource_Setup`, found under the `app/code/core/Mage/Core/Model/Resource/Setup.php` file
>
> `Varien_Db_Adapter_Pdo_Mysql`, found under the `lib/Varien/Db/Adapter/Pdo/Mysql.php` file

3. Now that we have defined our entities persistent storage and database table, we will go forward and define the entity itself. First, we need to create the `app/code/community/Foggyline/Logger/Model/Logger.php` file with the following code content:

```
<?php
class Foggyline_Logger_Model_Logger extends Mage_Core_Model_
Abstract
{
```

```
  protected function _construct()
  {
    $this->_init('foggyline_logger/logger');
  }
}
```

Code within the `Foggyline_Logger_Model_Logger` class is basic; we extend the `Mage_Core_Model_Abstract` class and define the `_construct()` method with a call towards the parent class `_init()` method, passing it the `'foggyline_logger/logger'` string parameter, which is basically a resource model path. All Magento data entities extend the `Mage_Core_Model_Abstract`. In this way they inherit all the logic required for proper functioning. Pay special attention to the name of the `_construct()` method; this is not your PHP constructor method.

4. Next, we create the `app/code/community/Foggyline/Logger/Model/Resource/Logger.php` resource file with the following code content:

```
<?php
class Foggyline_Logger_Model_Resource_Logger extends
  Mage_Core_Model_Resource_Db_Abstract
{
  protected function _construct()
  {
    $this->_init('foggyline_logger/logger', 'entity_id');
  }
}
```

The same as with the previous class file, we have a basic class with just a single method and a single statement within it. This time we are extending the `Mage_Core_Model_Resource_Db_Abstract` class whose `_init()` method takes two parameters. The first parameter, `'foggyline_logger/logger'`, matches the database table name, and the second parameter matches your entity database table primary key column name. Be sure to correctly pass the underscores and lower or uppercase names used in your `config.xml` file. Pay special attention to these parameters as they are often the cause of `my models are not working` issues during extension development.

5. Our last model definition file is the collection file. For this, we need to create the `app/code/community/Foggyline/Logger/Model/Resource/Logger/Collection.php` file with the following code content:

```
<?php
class Foggyline_Logger_Model_Resource_Logger_Collection
  extends Mage_Core_Model_Resource_Db_Collection_Abstract
{
  public function _construct()
  {
    $this->_init('foggyline_logger/logger');
  }
}
```

   We have a basic class with just a single method and a single statement within it. This time we are extending the `Mage_Core_Model_Resource_Db_Collection_Abstract` class whose `_init()` method takes one parameter, string `'foggyline_logger/logger'`, which stands for the model name.

> In order to grasp a deeper understanding of the code behind the model entity, you are strongly encouraged to spare some time and study the code within the `Mage_Core_Model_Abstract`, `Mage_Core_Model_Resource_Db_Abstract`, `Mage_Core_Model_Resource_Db_Collection_Abstract` class, and their parent classes.

6. Finally, this is just for the sake of Magento, we will create our helper file with the following code content:

```
<?php
class Foggyline_Logger_Helper_Data extends
  Mage_Core_Helper_Data
{
}
```

> In this case, we have a helper class that merely inherits from `Mage_Core_Helper_Data`, but does not implement any methods of its own. Its purpose is to provide extension scope translation.

Building the visual components

Now that we have defined our model and helper, we will proceed with defining the `Block` files that will render our logs under the Magento administration area, by performing the following steps:

1. First we add the block class group definition into our `config.xml` file, as shown in the following code:

```
<?xml version="1.0"?>
<config>
<!-- ...other elements... -->
  <global>
    <!-- ...other elements... -->
      <blocks>
        <foggyline_logger>
          <class>Foggyline_Logger_Block</class>
        </foggyline_logger>
      </blocks>
    <!-- ...other elements... -->
  </global>
<!-- ...other elements... -->
</config>
```

2. Once this is in place, we need to create two block-related classes. The first one is the `app/code/community/Foggyline/Logger/Block/Adminhtml/Edit.php` file with the following code content:

```
<?php
class Foggyline_Logger_Block_Adminhtml_Edit extends
  Mage_Adminhtml_Block_Widget_Grid_Container
{
  public function __construct()
  {
    $this->_blockGroup = 'foggyline_logger';
    $this->_controller = 'adminhtml_edit';
    $this->_headerText = Mage::helper('foggyline_logger')-
      >__('Logger - Log entries of everything that passed
        through Mage::log();');

    parent::__construct();

    $this->_removeButton('add');
  }
}
```

3. The second one is the app/code/community/Foggyline/Logger/Block/Adminhtml/Edit/Grid.php file with the following code content:

```
<?php
class Foggyline_Logger_Block_Adminhtml_Edit_Grid extends Mage_
Adminhtml_Block_Widget_Grid
{
  public function __construct()
  {
    parent::__construct();

    $this->setId('foggyline_logger');
    $this->setDefaultSort('entity_id');
    $this->setUseAjax(true);
  }

  protected function _prepareCollection()
  {
    $collection = Mage::getModel('foggyline_logger/logger')
    ->getCollection();

    $this->setCollection($collection);
    parent::_prepareCollection();
    return $this;
  }

  protected function _prepareColumns()
  {
    $this->addColumn('entity_id', array(
      'header' => Mage::helper('foggyline_logger')-
        >__('ID'),
      'sortable' => true,
      'index' => 'entity_id',
    ));

    $this->addColumn('timestamp', array(
      'header'    => Mage::helper('foggyline_logger')-
        >__('Timestamp'),
      'index'     => 'timestamp',
      'type'      => 'text',
      'width' => '170px',
    ));
```

```
    $this->addColumn('message', array(
      'header'    => Mage::helper('foggyline_logger')-
        >__('Message'),
      'index'     => 'message',
      'type'      => 'text',
    ));

    return parent::_prepareColumns();
  }

  public function getGridUrl()
  {
    return $this->getUrl('*/*/grid', array('_current' =>
      true));
  }
}
```

These two files (classes) go hand in hand with each other. The reason is that one extends the `Mage_Adminhtml_Block_Widget_Grid_Container` class and the other one extends the `Mage_Adminhtml_Block_Widget_Grid` class, which makes them parent and child.

> Grid classes, such as `Foggyline_Logger_Block_Adminhtml_Edit_Grid`, are usually pretty straightforward. You usually just need to implement the `__construct()`, `_prepareCollection()`, `_prepareColumns()`, `getGridUrl()` methods within them.

> A great self-study resource when it comes to grid blocks is the `app/code/core/Mage/Adminhtml/Block/` folder, and you can find all the `Grid.php` files under its subfolders.

4. Next, we add the `controller` file that will be used to render the blocks that we just defined previously, so we add the `app/code/community/Foggyline/Logger/controllers/Adminhtml/Foggyline/LoggerController.php` file with the following code content:

```
<?php
class Foggyline_Logger_Adminhtml_Foggyline_LoggerController
  extends Mage_Adminhtml_Controller_Action
{
  public function indexAction()
  {
```

```
        $this->loadLayout()-
          >_setActiveMenu('system/tools/foggyline_logger');
        $this->_addContent($this->getLayout()-
          >createBlock('foggyline_logger/adminhtml_edit'));
        $this->renderLayout();
    }

    public function gridAction()
    {
        $this->getResponse()->setBody(
          $this->getLayout()-
            >createBlock(
              'foggyline_logger/adminhtml_edit_grid')->toHtml()
        );
    }
}
```

5. The preceding file extends the `Mage_Adminhtml_Controller_Action` class, which makes it the admin controller. In order for Magento to react to it, we need to add a special entry to our `config.xml` file, as shown in the following code:

```
<?xml version="1.0"?>
<config>
  <!-- ...other elements... -->
    <admin>
      <routers>
        <adminhtml>
          <args>
            <modules>
              <Foggyline_Logger before="Mage_Adminhtml">
                Foggyline_Logger_Adminhtml
              </Foggyline_Logger>
            </modules>
          </args>
        </adminhtml>
      </routers>
    </admin>
  <!-- ...other elements... -->
</config>
```

6. And finally, we need a menu item with a link to our controller, which is done through the `app/code/community/Foggyline/Logger/etc/adminhtml.xml` file, by adding the following code content to it:

```
<?xml version="1.0"?>
<config>
  <menu>
    <system>
      <children>
        <tools>
          <children>
            <foggyline_logger translate="title"
              module="foggyline_logger">
              <title>Logger</title>
              <action>adminhtml/foggyline_logger/index
                </action>
              <sort_order>25</sort_order>
            </foggyline_logger>
          </children>
        </tools>
      </children>
    </system>
  </menu>
</config>
```

Now, if you log in to the Magento administration interface and navigate to **System | Tools | Logger**, you should see an empty grid. In case you see a 404 error, just log out and log back in again.

Adding the business logic

Finally, to make the whole thing work, we need to start recording our logs. To do so, we will overwrite the existing `log/core/writer_model` with our own, by performing the following steps:

1. We add the following rewrite definition under our existing `config.xml` file, by adding the following code:

```
<?xml version="1.0"?>
<config>
<!-- ...other elements... -->
  <global>
    <log>
      <core>
```

```
        <!--<writer_model>Zend_Log_Writer_Stream
          </writer_model>-->
        <writer_model>
          Foggyline_Logger_Model_Log_Writer_Stream
            </writer_model>
      </core>
    </log>
  </global>
<!-- ...other elements... -->
</config>
```

The previous rewrite definition is not the standard Magento model class rewrite. The `depends` tag within the `Foggyline_Logger.xml` file makes sure that the `Mage_Core` extension is loaded before the `Foggyline_Logger` extension. Then, this definition of `config/global/log/core/writer_model` simply overwrites the same one from `Mage_Core extension` during its configuration files merge process, as our extension is loaded after the `Mage_Core` extension.

2. Finally, we add the following code content to the `app/code/community/Foggyline/Logger/Model/Log/Writer/Stream.php` file:

```
<?php
class Foggyline_Logger_Model_Log_Writer_Stream extends
  Zend_Log_Writer_Stream
{
  /* foggyline logger file path */
  private static $_flfp;

  public function __construct($streamOrUrl, $mode = NULL)
  {
    self::$_flfp = $streamOrUrl;
    return parent::__construct($streamOrUrl, $mode);
  }

  protected function _write($event)
  {
    $logger = Mage::getModel('foggyline_logger/logger');

    $logger->setTimestamp($event['timestamp']);
    $logger->setMessage($event['message']);
    $logger->setPriority($event['priority']);
    $logger->setPriorityName($event['priorityName']);
```

```
        if (is_string(self::$_flfp)) {
          $logger->setFile(self::$_flfp);
        }

        try {
          $logger->save();
        } catch (Exception $e) {
          //echo $e->getMessage(); exit;
          /* Silently die... */
        }

        /* Now pass the execution to original parent code */
        return parent::_write($event);
      }
    }
```

In order to understand what's happening in our `Stream.php` file, we need to take a look inside the `Zend_Log_Writer_Stream` class. Our intention is to execute our part of the code at the moment Magento writes to a logfile. This moment is caught in the `_write($event)` method, which we are overriding with our own. Within the method, we are simply instantiating our `Logger` model, setting its properties via magic methods, and saving the model.

Summary

This chapter introduced the installation script, model entity, administration controller, grid block class, and a configuration rewrite, thus demonstrating simple, clean, yet powerful functionality that can be achieved in just a few lines of code. In *Chapter 4, Building the Extension – Shipping*, we will take a look at the Magento shipping methods, and learn how to code an extension for our custom shipping method.

4

Building the Extension – Shipping

The default Magento installation comes with several built-in shipping methods available: Flat Rate, Table Rates, Free Shipping UPS, USPS, FedEx, and DHL. For some merchants, this is more than enough; for others, you are free to build an additional custom shipping extension with support for one or more shipping methods. Be careful about the terminology here. Shipping method resides within shipping extension. A single extension can define one or more shipping methods. In this chapter, we will learn how to create our own shipping method.

Shipping methods

There are two, unofficially divided, types of shipping methods:

- Static, where the shipping cost rates are based on a predefined set of rules. For example, you can create a shipping method called 5+ and make it available to the customer for selection under the checkout only if they added more than five products to the cart.
- Dynamic, where retrieval of shipping cost rates comes from various shipping providers. For example, you have a web service called ABC Shipping that exposes a SOAP web service API which accepts products weight, length, height, width, shipping address, and returns the calculated shipping cost that you can then show to your customer.

Experienced developers would probably expect one or more PHP interfaces to handle the implementation of new shipping methods. The same goes for Magento, implementing a new shipping method is done via an interface and via proper configuration.

Planning your extension

Just the same as with the previous extensions we built, we first need to lay out some general plan for our shipping extension. We will build a simple shipping extension with a single shipping method that conforms to the following functionality:

- Will only be applicable to the customers who selected United States as a shipping country
- Will charge $20 for orders whose total value is below $100
- Will charge $10 for orders whose total value is above $100
- Will only be available for customers and not for admin users

Registering your extension

The following are the steps for registering your extension so that Magento can see it:

1. Prior to writing any real code, we first decide on a name for our extension. We will call it `Foggyline_Cargo`, and it will be placed under the community `codePool`.
2. Once we settle on a name, we go ahead and define an extension registration file, `app/etc/modules/Foggyline_Cargo.xml`, with the following content:

```
<?xml version="1.0" encoding="UTF-8"?>
<config>
    <modules>
        <Foggyline_Cargo>
            <active>true</active>
            <codePool>community</codePool>
            <depends>
                <Mage_Shipping/>
            </depends>
        </Foggyline_Cargo>
    </modules>
</config>
```

> With the `depends` tag, Magento offers you the ability to load another extension before yours, as it establishes a load order (or error) for the extension `config.xml`.

3. Once the file is in place, you need to confirm that Magento can see it under **System** | **Configuration** | **Advanced** | **Advanced**. You should see your extension appear on the Disable Module Output list.
4. Once you confirm that Magento sees your extension, go ahead and create the main configuration file with the following content:

```
<?xml version="1.0" encoding="UTF-8"?>
<config>
    <modules>
        <Foggyline_Cargo>
            <version>1.0.0.0</version>
        </Foggyline_Cargo>
    </modules>
</config>
```

Dissecting the existing shipping method

Magento defines its shipping methods, also called carriers, under the `config/default/carriers` XML element.

If you take a look at `app/code/core/Mage/Shipping/etc/config.xml`, you can see several carriers' definition as the one for the Flat Rate shipping method, as the following code:

```
<?xml version="1.0"?>
<config>
  <!-- ... -->
    <default>
      <carriers>
        <flatrate>
          <active>1</active>
          <sallowspecific>0</sallowspecific>
          <model>shipping/carrier_flatrate</model>
          <name>Fixed</name>
          <price>5.00</price>
          <title>Flat Rate</title>
          <type>I</type>
          <specificerrmsg>This shipping method is currently
            unavailable. If you would like to ship using this
              shipping method, please contact us.</specificerrmsg>
          <handling_type>F</handling_type>
        </flatrate>
      </carriers>
    </default>
  <!-- ... -->
</config>
```

Since the Flat Rate method bares one of the simplest shipping method functionalities with it, it is worth dissecting it a bit further. The most interesting part here is the `model` element definition whose value `shipping/carrier_flatrate` points to the `app/code/core/Mage/Shipping/Model/Carrier/Flatrate.php` class file. Taking a quick look at the `Flatrate.php` class file, as shown in the following code, reveals the magic behind the Magento shipping method:

```
<?php
class Mage_Shipping_Model_Carrier_Flatrate
  extends Mage_Shipping_Model_Carrier_Abstract
  implements Mage_Shipping_Model_Carrier_Interface
  {

    protected $_code = 'flatrate';
    protected $_isFixed = true;

    // ...
```

The interface `Mage_Shipping_Model_Carrier_Interface` is extremely simple, and it only asks you to define two methods: `isTrackingAvailable()` and `getAllowedMethods()`. The `isTrackingAvailable()` method is already defined within the extended `Mage_Shipping_Model_Carrier_Abstract` class. A quick look inside the `Mage_Shipping_Model_Carrier_Abstract` class reveals one bodiless abstract method, `collectRates(Mage_Shipping_Model_Rate_Request $request)`, which also must be implemented in our class.

Next to the definitions within the `config.xml` file, are several definitions related to shipping methods under the `system.xml` file that defines all the visually configurable options available under the Magento administration area. In the case of the Flat Rate shipping method these can be found under the `config/sections/carriers/groups/flatrate/fields` XML element of the `app/code/core/Mage/Shipping/etc/system.xml` file.

With regards our custom shipping method, a few things are clear from the preceding code:

- We will have to add a proper carrier definition under the `config/default/carriers` XML element, defining our own shipping method `model`
- We will have to extend from the `Mage_Shipping_Model_Carrier_Abstract` class
- We will have to write our own implementation of the `collectRates(Mage_Shipping_Model_Rate_Request $request)` method
- We will have to implement the `Mage_Shipping_Model_Carrier_Interface` interface

- We will have to write our own implementation of the `getAllowedMethods()` method
- We will mimic some of the configuration options defined in `system.xml` for `config/sections/carriers/groups/flatrate/fields`

> Using the Flat Rate shipping method code as a reference is a great starting point for your first shipping method.

Defining your shipping method

Now that we have a clear picture on different elements that comprise a single shipping method, let's define one, by performing the following steps:

1. Edit the `config.xml` file by adding the following code to it. This defines a model class group that we will use later for further defining the `config/default/carriers` XML element.

```
<?xml version="1.0" encoding="UTF-8"?>
<config>
  <!-- ... -->
  <global>
    <models>
        <foggyline_cargo>
          <class>Foggyline_Cargo_Model</class>
        </foggyline_cargo>
      </models>
  </global>
  <!-- ... -->
</config>
```

2. Edit the `config.xml` file by adding the following code to it. This adds the definition for our shipping method (carrier).

```
<?xml version="1.0" encoding="UTF-8"?>
<config>
  <!-- ... -->
    <default>
      <carriers>
        <foggyline_cargo_fixy>
          <active>1</active>
          <model>foggyline_cargo/shipping_carrier_fixy
            </model>
```

```
          <title>Foggyline Cargo</title>
          <name>Fixy</name>
        </foggyline_cargo_fixy>
      </carriers>
    </default>
  <!-- ... -->
</config>
```

The value `foggyline_cargo/shipping_carrier_fixy` of `config/default /carriers/foggyline_cargo/model` element tells us that Magento will try to load the `Foggyline_Cargo_Model_Shipping_Carrier_Fixy` class from within the `app/code/community/Foggyline/Cargo/Model/Shipping/Carrier/Fixy.php` file.

3. Create the `app/code/community/Foggyline/Cargo/etc/system.xml` file with the following content:

```
<?xml version="1.0"?>

<config>
  <sections>
    <carriers>
      <groups>
        <foggyline_cargo_fixy translate="label">
          <label>Foggyline Cargo Fixy</label>
          <frontend_type>text</frontend_type>
          <sort_order>999</sort_order>
          <show_in_default>1</show_in_default>
          <show_in_website>1</show_in_website>
          <show_in_store>1</show_in_store>
          <fields>
            <active translate="label">
              <label>Enabled</label>
              <frontend_type>select</frontend_type>
              <source_model>
                adminhtml/system_config_source_yesno
                  </source_model>
              <sort_order>1</sort_order>
              <show_in_default>1</show_in_default>
              <show_in_website>1</show_in_website>
              <show_in_store>0</show_in_store>
            </active>
            <title translate="label">
              <label>Title</label>
```

```
                <frontend_type>text</frontend_type>
                <sort_order>2</sort_order>
                <show_in_default>1</show_in_default>
                <show_in_website>1</show_in_website>
                <show_in_store>1</show_in_store>
              </title>
              <name translate="label">
                <label>Method Name</label>
                <frontend_type>text</frontend_type>
                <sort_order>3</sort_order>
                <show_in_default>1</show_in_default>
                <show_in_website>1</show_in_website>
                <show_in_store>1</show_in_store>
              </name>
            </fields>
          </foggyline_cargo_fixy>
        </groups>
      </carriers>
    </sections>
  </config>
```

Right now, if you open the Magento administration area and go to **System | Configuration | Sales | Shipping Methods** you should see a **Foggyline Cargo Fixy** method on the list, as shown in the following screenshot:

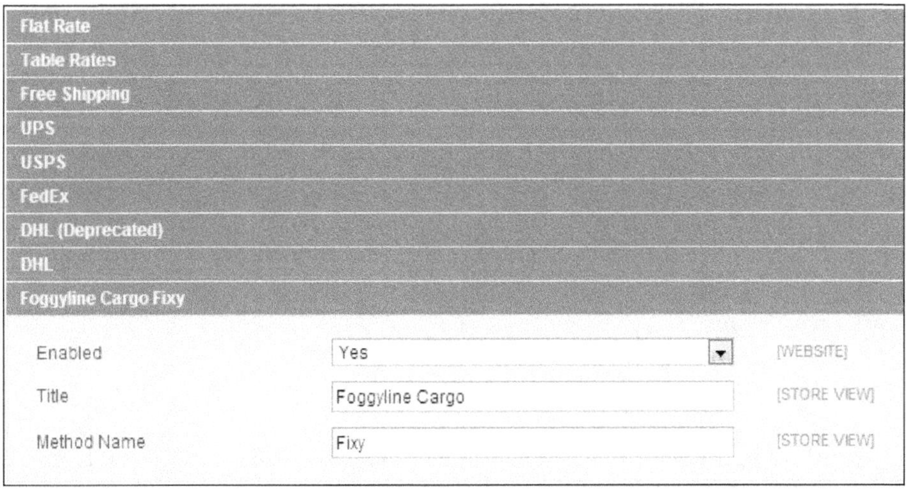

4. Create the `app/code/community/Foggyline/Cargo/Model/Shipping/Carrier/Fixy.php` file with the following initial content:

```
<?php
class Foggyline_Cargo_Model_Shipping_Carrier_Fixy
extends Mage_Shipping_Model_Carrier_Abstract
implements Mage_Shipping_Model_Carrier_Interface
{
  protected $_code = 'foggyline_cargo_fixy';

  public function
    collectRates(Mage_Shipping_Model_Rate_Request $request)
  {
    $result = Mage::getModel('shipping/rate_result');
    $method =
      Mage::getModel('shipping/rate_result_method');

    $method->setCarrier($this->_code);
    $method->setCarrierTitle($this-
      >getConfigData('title'));

    $method->setMethod($this->_code);
    $method->setMethodTitle($this->getConfigData('name'));

    $method->setPrice(14.99); /* temporary hard coded */
    $method->setCost(14.99); /* temporary hard coded */

    $result->append($method);

    return $result;
  }

  public function getAllowedMethods()
  {
    return array($this->_code => $this-
      >getConfigData('name'));
  }
}
```

Right now, if you add some products to the Magento cart on the frontend and try to do a checkout you should see your `Foggyline Cargo` method on the **Shipping Method** step as shown in the following screenshot:

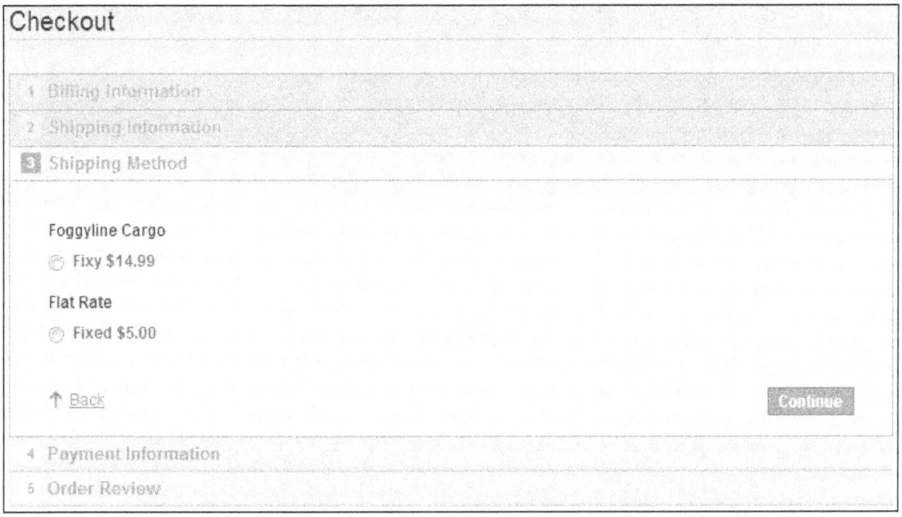

> There is no technical reason why we placed the `Fixy.php` file within `Model/Shipping/Carrier` folder and not directly within the `Model` folder. This was merely to follow a certain pattern of Magento, where later one might guess what the file is used for without even opening it.

Adding the business logic

If you successfully followed the previous instructions, you should now have a bare minimum shipping extension. Consider it a starting point for adding further business logic to it. Right now, our shipping method will always set the shipping price to $14.99, since this value is currently hardcoded into the code, and it will be applicable to customers from all states.

In order to achieve the `Will only be applicable to the customers who selected United States as a shipping country` functionality as planned, the following steps need to be performed:

1. Edit the `app/code/community/Foggyline/Cargo/etc/system.xml` file by adding the following two fields to it, right below the `name` field:

```
<allowspecific translate="label">
  <label>Ship to Applicable Countries</label>
  <frontend_type>select</frontend_type>
  <sort_order>90</sort_order>
```

```
        <frontend_class>shipping-applicable-
          country</frontend_class>
        <source_model>adminhtml/
          system_config_source_shipping_allspecificcountries
            </source_model>
        <show_in_default>1</show_in_default>
        <show_in_website>1</show_in_website>
        <show_in_store>0</show_in_store>
      </allowspecific>
      <specificcountry translate="label">
        <label>Ship to Specific Countries</label>
        <frontend_type>multiselect</frontend_type>
        <sort_order>91</sort_order>
        <source_model>
          adminhtml/system_config_source_country</source_model>
        <show_in_default>1</show_in_default>
        <show_in_website>1</show_in_website>
        <show_in_store>0</show_in_store>
        <can_be_empty>1</can_be_empty>
      </specificcountry>
```

> There are lot of things that Magento does internally just by looking for the existence of certain XML elements within configuration files. In this case, Magento sees `allowspecific` and `specificcountry` field elements, and adds certain logic to your shipping method code, creating the select and multiselect input fields in the backend.

2. Open the Magento administration interface, navigate to **System** | **Configuration** | **Sales** | **Shipping Methods** | **Foggyline Cargo Fixy**, then set the newly available **Ship to Applicable Countries** option to **Specific Countries** value and **Ship to Specific Countries** option to **United States** value. Only then click on the **Save Config** button.
3. Navigate to the frontend checkout page, and try to change your shipping address to some country other than **United States**. Once you get to the **Shipping Method** step, the **Foggyline Cargo Fixy** method should not be available any more.

In order to achieve the `Will charge $20 for orders whose total value is below $100 and Will charge $10 for orders whose total value is above $100` functionality as planned, the following steps need to be performed:

1. Edit the `app/code/community/Foggyline/Cargo/Model/Shipping/Carrier/Fixy.php` file by changing the entire `collectRates` method body as shown in the following code:

```
public function
  collectRates(Mage_Shipping_Model_Rate_Request $request)
{
  $shippingPrice = 20;
  $grandTotal = Mage::getModel('checkout/session')
  ->getQuote()
  ->getGrandTotal();

  if ($grandTotal > 100) {
    $shippingPrice = 10;
  }

  $result = Mage::getModel('shipping/rate_result');
  $method = Mage::getModel('shipping/rate_result_method');

  $method->setCarrier($this->_code);
  $method->setCarrierTitle($this->getConfigData('title'));

  $method->setMethod($this->_code);
  $method->setMethodTitle($this->getConfigData('name'));

  $mthod->setPrice($shippingPrice);
  $method->setCost($shippingPrice);

  $result->append($method);

  return $result;
}
```

The essence of the code lies in getting the cart's grand total value. Take some experience or code tracing to know that this can be fetched by the `Mage::getModel('checkout/session')->getQuote()->getGrandTotal();` statement. After you obtain the grand total, the rest is basic PHP knowledge. Additionally, the store might have taxes configured, so additional logic might be needed to extract the tax-free grand total price.

2. Navigate to the frontend, and try adding some products to the cart in order to test the functionality. On the **Shipping Method** checkout step, you should be able to see the $10 shipping price for orders above $100, and the $20 shipping price for orders below $100.

In order to achieve the `Will only be available on the frontend, not in the administration area` functionality as planned, the following steps need to be performed:

1. Edit the `app/code/community/Foggyline/Cargo/Model/Shipping/Carrier/Fixy.php` file by modifying the section of the `collectRates` method body as shown in the following code:

```
public function
  collectRates(Mage_Shipping_Model_Rate_Request $request)
{
  if (!$this->getConfigFlag('active') ||
    Mage::app()->getStore()->isAdmin()) {
    return false;
  }

  $shippingPrice = 20;
  $grandTotal = Mage::getModel('checkout/session')
  ->getQuote()
  ->getGrandTotal();

  //...
```

   Here we are covering two things actually. First, we are adding the general extension, that is active or inactive logic via the use of the `!$this->getConfigFlag('active')` statement. This works in conjunction with our `system.xml active` configuration option, which can be set to **Enabled** or **Disabled** by the admin user. Secondly, we are conforming to the functional requirement itself via the use of the `Mage::app()->getStore()->isAdmin()` statement.

2. Confirm that you can still see the **Foggyline Cargo Fixy** method on the frontend **Shipping Method checkout** step.

3. Confirm that you cannot see the **Foggyline Cargo Fixy** method on the administration area during the order creation process available under the **Sales | Orders | Create New Order** screens, under the **Shipping Method** box.

If you successfully executed all the steps, you should now have a minimal, but fully functional shipping extension. Although simple, the functionality of this extension can be greatly extended just by implementing further business logic into the `collectRates` method and by studying the core shipping methods code.

Summary

In this chapter, we learned the basics of the Magento shipping method implementation. Based on that, we built our own simple shipping method that further implemented several business rules. Our extension was built with a presumption of using the default Magento installation with USD ($) currency only and no tax configured. When building an extension for distributing, you will need to dig a bit deeper into it, covering the currency and tax calculations. Since the focus of this chapter was on overall introduction and a basic shipping example, we leave it up to you to handle more complex shipping methods.

In *Chapter 5, Building the Extension - Payment,* we will familiarize ourselves with payment methods and build a payment extension.

5
Building the Extension – Payment

The default Magento installation comes with several built-in payment methods available: PayPal, Saved CC, Check/Money Order, Zero Subtotal Checkout, Bank Transfer Payment, Cash On Delivery payment, Purchase Order, and Authorize. Net. For some merchants this is more than enough. Various additional payment extensions can be found on Magento Connect. For those that do not yet exist, you are free to build an additional custom payment extension with support for one or more payment methods. Building a payment extension is usually a non-trivial task that requires a lot of focus.

Payment methods

There are several unofficially divided types of payment method implementations such as redirect payment, hosted (on-site) payment, and an embedded iframe. Two of them stand out as the most commonly used ones:

- **Redirect payment**: During the checkout, once the customer reaches the final **ORDER REVIEW** step, he/she clicks on the **Place Order** button. Magento then redirects the customer to specific payment provider website where the customer is supposed to provide the credit card information and execute the actual payment. What's specific about this is that prior to redirection, Magento needs to create the order in the system, and it does so by assigning this new order a **Pending** status. Later, if the customer provides the valid credit card information on the payment provider website, the customer gets redirected back to the Magento success page. The main concept to grasp here is that the customer might just close the payment provider website and never return to your store, leaving your order indefinitely in a **Pending** status. The great thing about this redirect type of payment method providers (gateways) is that they are relatively easy to implement in Magento.

- **Hosted (on-site) payment**: Unlike redirect payment, there is no redirection here. Everything is handled on the Magento store. During the checkout, once the customer reaches the **Payment Information** step, he/she is presented with a form for providing the credit card information. After which, when he/she clicks on the **Place Order** button in the last **ORDER REVIEW** checkout step, Magento then internally calls the appropriate payment provider web service, passing it the billing information. Depending on the web service response, Magento then internally sets the order status to either **Processing** or some other. For example, this payment provider; web service can be a standard SOAP service with a few methods such as `orderSubmit`. Additionally, we don't even have to use a real payment provider, we can just make a "dummy" payment implementation such as a built-in Check/Money Order payment. You will often find that most of the merchants prefer this type of payment method, as they believe that redirecting the customer to a third-party site might negatively affect their sale. Obviously, with this payment method there is more overhead for you as a developer to handle the implementation. On top of that there are security concerns of handling the credit card data on the Magento side, in which case PCI compliance is obligatory. If this is your first time hearing about PCI compliance, please see `https://www.pcisecuritystandards.org` for more information about it. This type of payment method is slightly more challenging to implement than the redirect payment method.

Planning your extension

Within this chapter we will build a payment extension for the Stripe payment gateway available at `https://stripe.com`. Unlike some other payment gateways, Stripe is fully developer-friendly, well-documented, and easy to implement. If you haven't already, now is the good time to:

1. Visit the Stripe web page and sign up for an account.
2. Once you sign up, follow the Stripe documentation for obtaining the API key (`https://manage.stripe.com/account/apikeys`). You will need a test secret key, which we will use later within Magento.
3. Additionally, you will need to obtain the PHP API library (`stripe-php-latest.zip`) available at `https://stripe.com/docs/libraries`. Once you unpack the downloaded archive, there should be a `VERSION` file in it. The current version at the time of this writing is 1.8.0.
4. Spend some time studying/navigating the documentation page, `https://stripe.com/docs/tutorials/checkout`, just to get an overview of things.

Please note that actual URLs might change throughout time. Once you are done with the previously mentioned steps, we can proceed with actual extension development.

Registering your extension

The steps for registering your extension, so that Magento can see it, are as follows:

1. Prior to writing any real code, we first decide on a name for our extension. We will call it `Foggyline_Stripe`, and it will be placed under the community `codePool`.
2. Once we settle on a name, we go ahead and define an extension registration file, `app/etc/modules/Foggyline_Stripe.xml`, with the following code snippet:

```
<?xml version="1.0" encoding="UTF-8"?>
<config>
    <modules>
        <Foggyline_Stripe>
            <active>true</active>
            <codePool>community</codePool>
            <depends>
                <Mage_Payment/>
            </depends>
        </Foggyline_Stripe>
    </modules>
</config>
```

3. Once the file is in place, you need to confirm that Magento can see it under **System** | **Configuration** | **Advanced** | **Advanced**. You should see your extension appear on the **Disable Extension Output** list.
4. Once you confirm that Magento sees your extension, go ahead and create the main configuration `app/code/community/Foggyline/Stripe/etc/config.xml` file with the following code snippet:

```
<?xml version="1.0" encoding="UTF-8"?>
<config>
    <modules>
        <Foggyline_Stripe>
            <version>1.0.0.0</version>
        </Foggyline_Stripe>
    </modules>
</config>
```

Dissecting the existing payment method

Magento defines its payment methods across multiple extensions. For example, dummy payment methods such as Saved CC, Check/Money Order, Zero Subtotal Checkout, Bank Transfer Payment, Cash On Delivery payment, and Purchase Order are defined within the `Mage_Payment` core extension, that is, under the `config` | `default` | `payment` XML element of the `app/code/core/Mage/Payment/etc/config.xml` file. The remaining two, PayPal and Authorize.Net, are each defined within its own separate extension (`Mage_Paypal`, `Mage_PaypalUk`, `Mage_Authorizenet`).

If you took some time to study the Stripe documentation, you could have concluded that Stripe enables you to execute the payments right from your site, which would position our extension as a hosted (on-site) payment method. If you think further, accepting credit card payments on-site is something that the built-in Saved CC payment method already does, even though it has no real web service API link in the background. What it does have is the credit card data collecting form on the checkout as shown in the following screenshot:

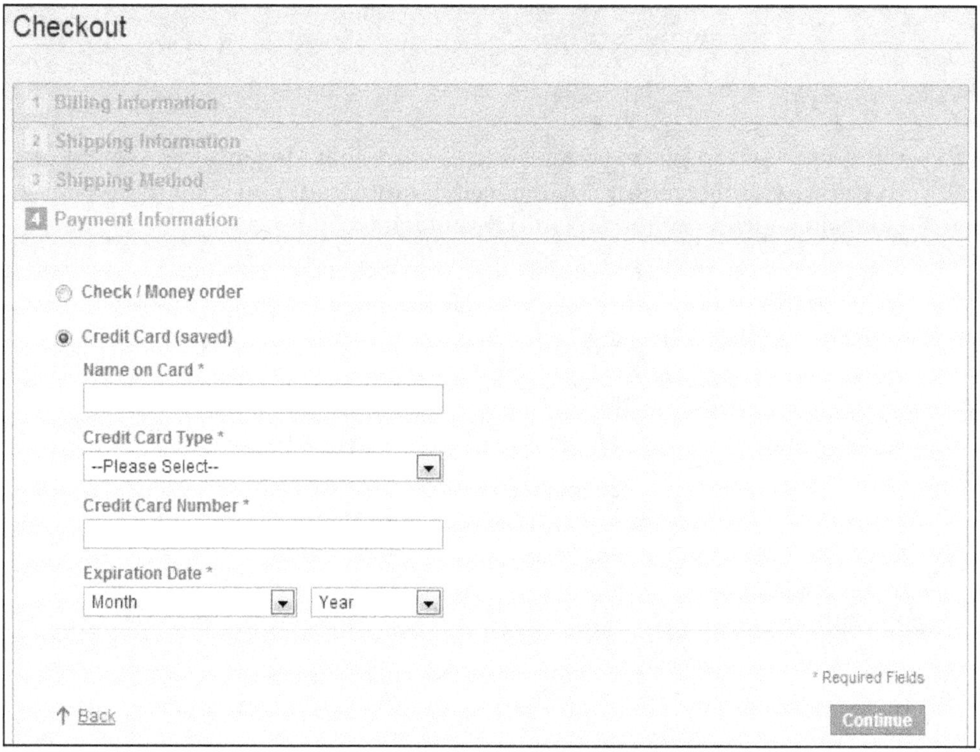

This form is basically a generic form for any credit card data collecting payment provider, so it fits perfectly into what we will need for Stripe. All of this makes dissecting Saved CC a starting point for our new extension. Now, let's take a look at the definition of Saved CC as shown in the following `app/code/core/Mage/Payment/etc/config.xml` file:

```
<?xml version="1.0"?>
<config>
    <!-- ... -->
    <default>
    <!-- ... -->
        <payment>
        <!-- ... -->
            <ccsave>
                <active>1</active>
                <cctypes>AE,VI,MC,DI</cctypes>
                <model>payment/method_ccsave</model>
                <order_status>pending</order_status>
                <title>Credit Card (saved)</title>
                <allowspecific>0</allowspecific>
                <group>offline</group>
            </ccsave>
            <!-- ... -->
```

The most interesting part here is the model element definition whose value `payment/method_ccsave` points to the `app/code/core/Mage/Payment/Model/Method/Ccsave.php` class file. Taking a quick look at the `Ccsave.php` class file, as shown in the following code snippet, reveals the magic behind the Magento payment method:

```
class Mage_Payment_Model_Method_Ccsave extends Mage_Payment_Model_
Method_Cc
{
    protected $_code = 'ccsave';
    protected $_canSaveCc = true;
    protected $_formBlockType = 'payment/form_ccsave';
    protected $_infoBlockType = 'payment/info_ccsave';
}
```

The class `Mage_Payment_Model_Method_Ccsave` extends the `Mage_Payment_Model_Method_Cc` class, which further extends the essential payment class, `Mage_Payment_Model_Method_Abstract`. In order to be a successful Magento payment extension developer, you need to have a deep understanding of the inner workings of the `Mage_Payment_Model_Method_Abstract` class and the methods it declares. Magento internally uses these methods through various steps of the checkout process. Some of the most important methods are as follows:

- `authorize(Varien_Object $payment, $amount)`
- `capture(Varien_Object $payment, $amount)`
- `refund(Varien_Object $payment, $amount)`
- `cancel(Varien_Object $payment)`

In regards to our Stripe payment method, a few things are clear from the previous code:

- We will have to add a proper payment definition under the `config` | `default` | `payment` XML element, defining our own payment method model
- We will have to extend from the `Mage_Payment_Model_Method_Ccsave` class which will provide the full set of form fields for us
- We will have to write our own implementation of the `capture(Varien_Object $payment, $amount)` method (for the sake of simplicity, we will not implement the `authorize`, `refund`, and `cancel` methods)
- We will mimic some of the configuration options defined in `system.xml` for `config` | `sections` | `payment` | `groups` | `ccsave` | `fields`

> Using the Saved CC payment method code as a reference is a great starting point for your first credit card accepting payment method.

Defining your payment method

Now that we have a clear picture on different elements that comprise the single payment method, let's define one:

1. Edit the `app/code/community/Foggyline/Stripe/etc/config.xml` file by adding the following code to it. This defines a model class group that we will use later for further defining the `config` | `default` | `payment` XML element and a helper class group.

```
<?xml version="1.0" encoding="UTF-8"?>
<config>
    <!-- ... -->
    <global>
        <models>
            <foggyline_stripe>
                <class>Foggyline_Stripe_Model</class>
            </foggyline_stripe>
        </models>
        <helpers>
            <foggyline_stripe>
                <class>Foggyline_Stripe_Helper</class>
            </foggyline_stripe>
        </helpers>
    </global>
    <!-- ... -->
```

2. Edit the `app/code/community/Foggyline/Stripe/etc/config.xml` file by adding the following code to it. This adds the definition for our Stripe payment method.

```
<?xml version="1.0" encoding="UTF-8"?>
<config>
    <!-- ... -->
    <default>
        <payment>
            <foggyline_stripe>
                <model>foggyline_stripe/payment</model>
                <api_key
                  backend_model="adminhtml/system_config_backend_
                  encrypted"/>
                <payment_action>authorize_capture</payment_action>
                <title>Foggyline Stripe</title>
                <cctypes>AE,VI,MC,DI,JCB</cctypes>
                <useccv>1</useccv>
            </foggyline_stripe>
        </payment>
    </default>
    <!-- ... -->
```

3. The value `foggyline_stripe/payment` of `config | default | payment | foggyline_stripe | model` element tells us that Magento will try to load the `Foggyline_Stripe_Model_Payment` from within the `app/code/community/Foggyline/Stripe/Model/Payment.php` file.

4. Create the `app/code/community/Foggyline/Stripe/etc/system.xml` file with the following code snippet:

```
<?xml version="1.0" encoding="UTF-8"?>

<config>
    <sections>
        <payment>
            <groups>
                <foggyline_stripe>
                    <label>Foggyline Stripe</label>
                    <frontend_type>text</frontend_type>
                    <sort_order>999</sort_order>
                    <show_in_default>1</show_in_default>
                    <show_in_website>1</show_in_website>
                    <show_in_store>1</show_in_store>
                    <fields>
                        <active>
                            <label>Enabled</label>
                            <frontend_type>select</frontend_type>
                            <source_model>adminhtml/system_config_
                              source_yesno</source_model>
                            <sort_order>10</sort_order>
                            <show_in_default>1</show_in_default>
                            <show_in_website>1</show_in_website>
                            <show_in_store>0</show_in_store>
                        </active>
                        <title>
                            <label>Title</label>
                            <frontend_type>text</frontend_type>
                            <sort_order>15</sort_order>
                            <show_in_default>1</show_in_default>
                            <show_in_website>1</show_in_website>
                            <show_in_store>1</show_in_store>
                        </title>
                        <api_key>
                            <label>Api Key</label>
                            <frontend_type>obscure</frontend_type>
                            <backend_model>adminhtml/system_
                              config_backend_encrypted</backend_
                              model>
```

```
        <sort_order>20</sort_order>
        <show_in_default>1</show_in_default>
        <show_in_website>1</show_in_website>
        <show_in_store>0</show_in_store>
    </api_key>
    <debug>
        <label>Debug</label>
        <frontend_type>select</frontend_type>
        <source_model>adminhtml/system_config_
          source_yesno</source_model>
        <sort_order>25</sort_order>
        <show_in_default>1</show_in_default>
        <show_in_website>1</show_in_website>
        <show_in_store>0</show_in_store>
    </debug>
    <cctypes>
        <label>Credit Card
            Types</label>
        <frontend_type>multiselect</frontend_
          type>
        <source_model>foggyline_stripe/source_
          cctype</source_model>
        <sort_order>30</sort_order>
        <show_in_default>1</show_in_default>
        <show_in_website>1</show_in_website>
        <show_in_store>0</show_in_store>
    </cctypes>
    <useccv>
        <label>Credit Card
          Verification</label>
        <frontend_type>select</frontend_type>
        <source_model>adminhtml/system_config_
          source_yesno</source_model>
        <sort_order>35</sort_order>
        <show_in_default>1</show_in_default>
        <show_in_website>1</show_in_website>
        <show_in_store>0</show_in_store>
    </useccv>
```

```
                        <allowspecific>
                            <label>Payment from Applicable
                              Countries</label>
                            <frontend_type>allowspecific</
                              frontend_type>
                            <sort_order>40</sort_order>
                            <source_model>adminhtml/system_config_
                              source_payment_
                              allspecificcountries</source_model>
                            <show_in_default>1</show_in_default>
                            <show_in_website>1</show_in_website>
                            <show_in_store>0</show_in_store>
                        </allowspecific>
                        <specificcountry>
                            <label>Payment from Specific
                              Countries</label>
                            <frontend_type>multiselect</frontend_
                              type>
                            <sort_order>45</sort_order>
                            <source_model>adminhtml/system_config_
                              source_country</sourc  e_model>
                            <show_in_default>1</show_in_default>
                            <show_in_website>1</show_in_website>
                            <show_in_store>0</show_in_store>
                            <depends>
                                <allowspecific>1</allowspecific>
                            </depends>
                        </specificcountry>
                    </fields>
                </foggyline_stripe>
            </groups>
        </payment>
    </sections>
</config>
```

5. Right now, if you open the Magento administration area and navigate to **System** | **Configuration** | **Sales** | **Payment Methods**, you should see a **Foggyline Stripe** method on the list as shown in the following screenshot:

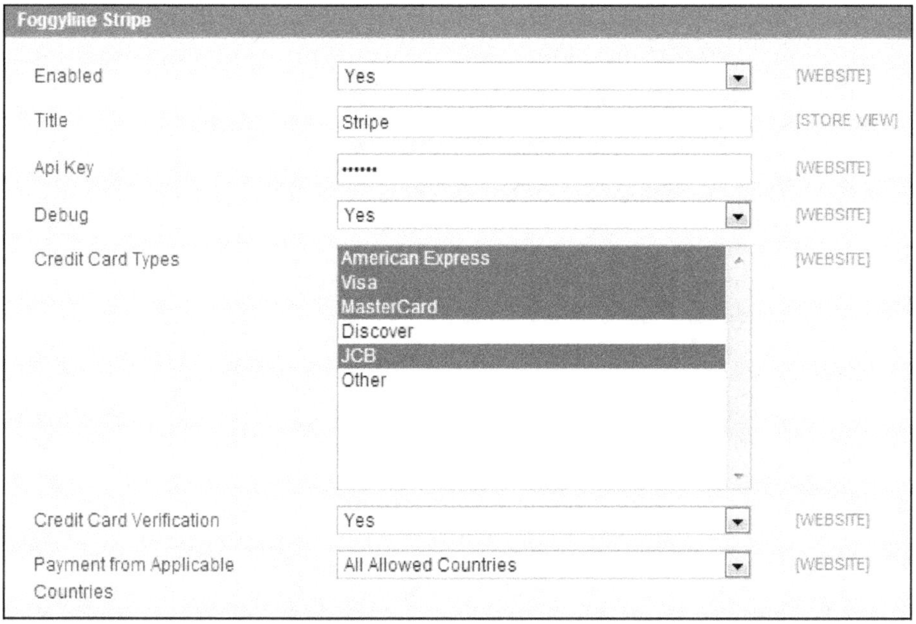

6. Now create the `lib` folder within the `app/code/community/Foggyline/Stripe` folder, and unpack the Stripe PHP API library within it, so that the `Stripe.php` file is available at the path `app/code/community/Foggyline/Stripe/lib/Stripe.php`. Right next to the `Stripe.php` file there should be additional `Stripe` and `data` folders.

7. Create the `app/code/community/Foggyline/Stripe/Helper/Data.php` file with the following code snippet, as it is needed for Magento, even though it is an empty class:

```
<?php
class Foggyline_Stripe_Helper_Data extends
  Mage_Payment_Helper_Data
{
}
```

8. Create the `app/code/community/Foggyline/Stripe/Model/Source/Cctype.php` file with the following code snippet:

```
<?php
class Foggyline_Stripe_Model_Source_Cctype extends
  Mage_Payment_Model_Source_Cctype
{
    protected $_allowedTypes =
      array('AE','VI','MC','DI','JCB','OT');
}
```

9. Create the `app/code/community/Foggyline/Stripe/Model/Payment.php` file with the following code snippet:

```
<?php
require_once dirname(__FILE__).'/../lib/Stripe.php';

class Foggyline_Stripe_Model_Payment extends
  Mage_Payment_Model_Method_Cc
{
    protected $_code = 'foggyline_stripe';
    protected $_isGateway = true;
    protected $_canCapture = true;
    protected $_supportedCurrencyCodes = array('USD');
    protected $_minOrderTotal = 0.5;

    public function __construct()
    {
        Stripe::setApiKey($this->getConfigData('api_key'));
    }

    public function capture(Varien_Object $payment,
      $amount)
    {
        $order = $payment->getOrder();
        $billingAddress = $order->getBillingAddress();

        try {
            $charge = Stripe_Charge::create(array(
                'amount' => $amount * 100,
                'currency' => strtolower($order-
                  >getBaseCurrencyCode()),
                'card' => array(
                    'number' => $payment->getCcNumber(),
                    'exp_month' => sprintf('%02d',
                      $payment->getCcExpMonth()),
                    'exp_year' => $payment->getCcExpYear(),
                    'cvc' => $payment->getCcCid(),
                    'name' => $billingAddress->getName(),
                    'address_line1' => $billingAddress-
                      >getStreet(1),
                    'address_line2' => $billingAddress-
                      >getStreet(2),
                    'address_zip' => $billingAddress-
                      >getPostcode(),
```

```
                    'address_state' => $billingAddress-
                      >getRegion(),
                    'address_country' => $billingAddress-
                      >getCountry(),
                ),
                'description' => sprintf('#%s, %s', $order-
                  >getIncrementId(), $order-
                  >getCustomerEmail())
            ));
        } catch (Exception $e) {
            $this->debugData($e->getMessage());
            Mage::throwException(Mage::helper('foggyline_sprite')-
>__('Payment capturing error.'));
        }

        $payment->setTransactionId($charge->id)
            ->setIsTransactionClosed(0);

        return $this;
    }

    public function isAvailable($quote = null)
    {
        if ($quote && $quote->getBaseGrandTotal() < $this-
          >_minOrderTotal) {
            return false;
        }

        return $this->getConfigData('api_key', ($quote ?
          $quote->getStoreId() : null)) &&
          parent::isAvailable($quote);
    }

    public function canUseForCurrency($currencyCode)
    {
        if (!in_array($currencyCode, $this-
          >_supportedCurrencyCodes)) {
            return false;
        }

        return true;
    }

}
```

10. Add some products to the cart and then go to the checkout. Confirm you can see your payment method on the **Payment Information** checkout step as shown in the following screenshot:

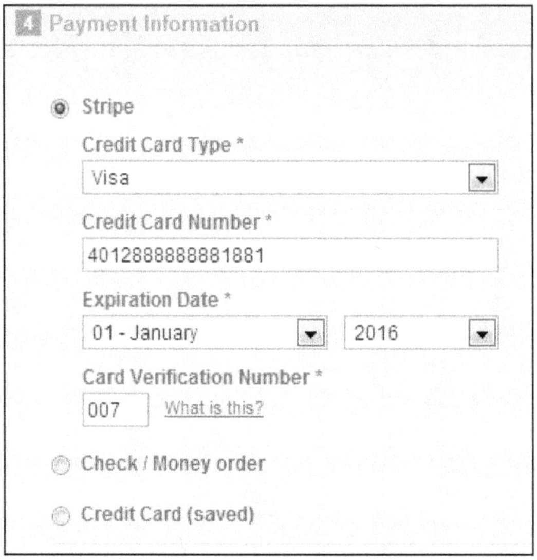

11. Once you click on the **Place Order** button in the final **ORDER REVIEW** checkout step and you get to the order success page, you should be able to see your order on the Stripe dashboard page under **GENERAL** | **Payments** as well, as shown in the following screenshot:

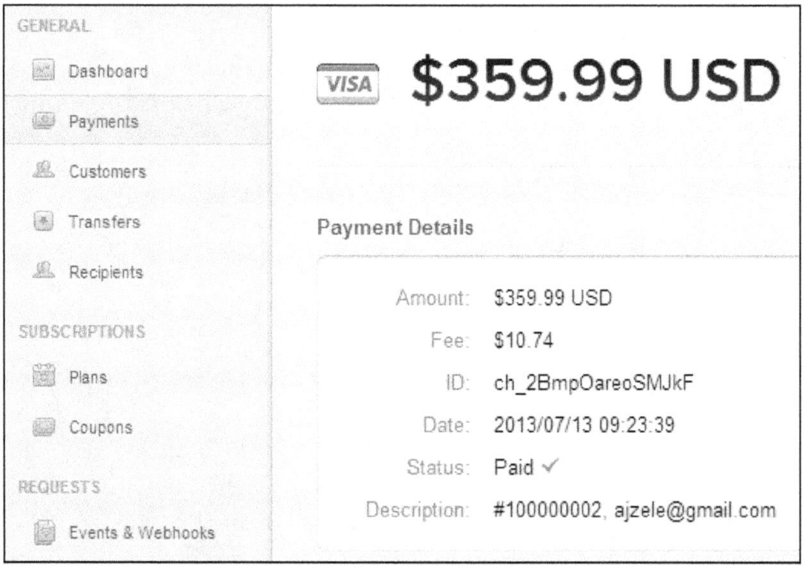

Extension business logic

In our extension, entire business logic is contained within a single `app/code/community/Foggyline/Stripe/Model/Payment.php` file. We are including the external Stripe library via the `require_once dirname(__FILE__).'/../lib/Stripe.php';` statement. Then we are implementing the `Stripe_Charge::create API` call within the capture method, passing it the customer and credit card information. Since we are using the Stripe PHP library, there is not much of the code we need to write ourselves, so the implementation is pretty short and clean.

If you successfully executed all the previous steps, you should now have a functional payment extension. Although simple, functionality of this extension can be further extended by adding the rest of the methods such as `authorize`, `refund`, and `cancel`. Authorize action is actually already contained within the `capture` method, but sometimes you might want to first authorize the payment then later manually capture it.

Summary

In this chapter we learned the basics of the Magento payment method implementation. Based on that we built our own simple payment method. Same as with the shipping extension, our extension was built with a presumption of using the default Magento installation with only USD ($) currency and no tax configuration.

When building an extension for distributing, you will need to dig a bit deeper into it, covering the currency and tax calculations.

In the next chapter we will learn how to package and distribute your extensions.

6

Packaging and Publishing Your Extension

Until now, we have learned some of the more important inner workings of the Magento platform, through theory and a few practical extensions. Once you get comfortable with building new extensions, you will most likely start thinking of sharing or selling them. If so, then Magento Connect should interest you.

Magento Connect

Magento Connect is one of the world's largest e-commerce application marketplaces where you can find various extensions to customize and enhance your Magento store.

It allows Magento community members and partners to share their open source or commercial contributions for Magento with the community.

You can access the Magento Connect marketplace at `http://www.magentocommerce.com/magento-connect url.`

Publishing your extension to Magento Connect is a three-step process, consisting of of the following steps:

1. Packaging your extension.
2. Creating an extension profile.
3. Uploading the extension package.

We'll discuss this process in detail later in the chapter.

Only the community members and partners have the ability to publish their contributions.

Becoming a community member is simple; just register as a user on the official Magento website, `https://www.magentocommerce.com`. A member account is a requirement for further packaging and publishing of your extension.

Those who are interested in becoming a partner should check out the information provided by Magento at `http://www.magentocommerce.com/partners`.

Free extensions versus commercial extensions

Free, sometimes called community extensions, are open source extensions created by Magento community members or partners that are released under an open source license. Please note that the community term, in this case, is not related to the code pool community.

Commercial extensions are the extensions that are available for purchase by Magento community members or partners. Commercial extensions may be sold, distributed, and licensed directly through the seller.

If you are building a commercial extension, you should be aware that Magento Connect does not actually do sales for you on its website. You can still list commercial extensions on connect, but for that you will have to provide the payment and delivery of the extension code through your own web store. Anyone interested in purchasing your commercial extension gets redirected to your web store.

Packaging your extension

The first step in publishing your extension is to package and upload it to the Magento Connect marketplace. For the purpose of packaging, we will choose our `Foggyline_Stripe` extension that we have in *Chapter 5, Building the Extension – Payment*.

Packaging an extension in Magento is done directly from its administration panel, as described in the following steps:

1. Log in to your Magento administration panel.
2. From the administration panel, navigate to **System** | **Magento Connect** | **Package Extensions**. This will take you to the **New Extension** page, as shown in the following screenshot:

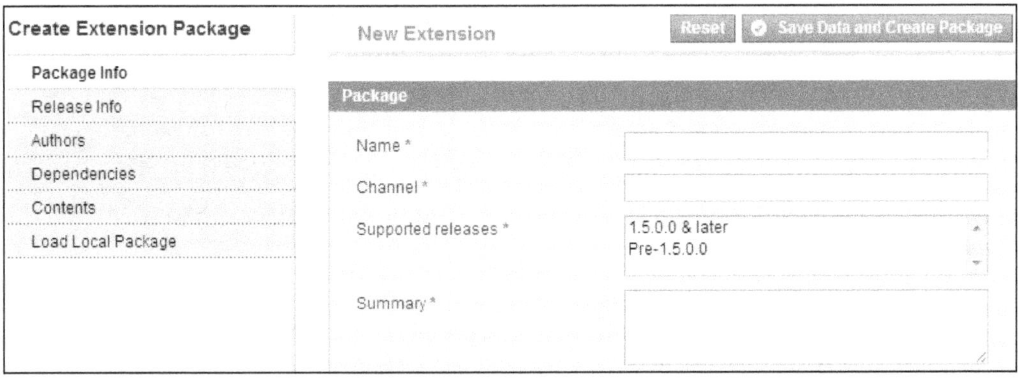

3. The **Create Extension Package** area of the **New Extension** page is made up of the following six sections:
   - Package info
   - Release info
   - Authors
   - Dependencies
   - Contents
   - Load Local Package

   We start off by filling the first opened section, the **Package info** section, as described in the following list, where most of the fields are required:

   - **Name** is a required field. It is a good practice to keep the name as a combination of your `Vendor Namespace` and `Module Name`. This value is not set in the store. Once you actually upload a packed extension to Magento Connect, you will once more provide an extension name there. For now, let's set this value to `Foggyline_Stripe`.
   - **Channel** is a required field. `Channel community` is used for Magento Version 1.5, or later. Since the examples in this book were written for Magento 1.7, we will use `community` for the **Channel** value.
   - **Supported releases** is a required field. Select the **1.5.0.0 & later** option.
   - **Summary** is a required field. Provide a brief summary about your extension.
   - **Description** is a required field. Provide a brief description about your extension.

   - **License** is a required field. Select the license that your extension falls under; it's a free-form entry, for example OSL v3.0.
   - **License URL** is an optional field. For OSL v3.0, the license that we set in the previous field, `http://opensource.org/licenses/osl-3.0.php`. The license URL should match the selected license.

4. Switch to the **Release info** section, then fill in the fields as follows:
   - **Release Version** is a required field. You should set its value to the same value you have in your extension `config.xml` file under the `config/extensions/Foggyline_Stripe/version` element, which is 1.0.0. You can check out the `http://semver.org` website for more information on forming the version number.
   - **Release Stability** is a required field. You can choose from several values such as **Development**, **Alpha**, **Beta**, and **Stable**. Extensions with **Development** release stability will not be approved; this option is used for testing purposes only. Keep in mind that by default, Magento Connect users are only allowed to install `Stable` release extensions. Choose **Stable**.
   - **Notes** is a required field. You can add any notes you may have for this release. Let's put something as `First stable release of Foggyline_Stripe`.

5. Switch to the **Authors** section. Within this section, you are supposed to add information about all the members who contributed to this extension. Proceed with entering your own details for **Name**, **User**, and **Email**.
   - The **Name** field value should contain your full name, for example `John Doe`.
   - The **User** field value should contain your Magento Connect account username, the one you have been assigned, once you log in to `https://www.magentocommerce.com`, for example `john_doe`.
   - The **Email** field value should contain your Magento Connect account's e-mail address, for example `john_doe@example.com`.

6. Switch to the **Dependencies** section. Here, you will see three distinctive field sets, namely **PHP Version**, **Packages**, and **Extensions**. Besides a minimum and maximum required PHP version, Magento allows you to define dependence on other Magento extensions, or PHP libraries, such as GD library. Proceed with just setting the **Minimum** to `5.2.0` and **Maximum** to `6.0.0` PHP version values.

7. Switch to the **Contents** section. This is one of the most important sections in the extension packaging process. Take extreme caution while filling its required fields, because it's easy to mess up.

   When you click on the **Add Contents Path** button, a new row of the following input fields appears: **Target**, **Path**, **Type**, **Include**, and **Ignore**.

   It is essential that you understand the following values offered under the **Target** drop-down menu:

   - **Magento Local module file**: It refers to the `./app/code/local` directory
   - **Magento Community module file**: It refers to the `./app/code/community` directory
   - **Magento Core team module file**: It refers to the `./app/code/core` directory
   - **Magento User Interface (layouts, templates)**: It refers to the `./app/design` directory
   - **Magento Global Configuration**: It refers to the `./app/etc` directory
   - **Magento PHP Library file**: It refers to the `./lib` directory
   - **Magento Locale language file**: It refers to the `./app/locale` directory
   - **Magento Media library**: It refers to the `./media` directory
   - **Magento Theme Skin (Images, CSS, JS)**: It refers to the `./skin` directory
   - **Magento Other web accessible file**: It refers to the `./` directory
   - **Magento PHPUnit test**: It refers to the `./tests` directory
   - **Magento other**: It refers to the `./` directory

   In the preceding list string, ./ represents the Magento root directory.

   Once you understand what **Target** value presents, it's easy to fill in the **Path** field. All you have to do is to think about which files and folders your extension is using. If we look back at our `Foggyline_Stripe`, the following are the files and folders it uses:

   - `app/code/community/Foggyline/Stripe/`
   - `app/etc/modules/Foggyline_Stripe.xml`

8. Now, fill in the first row of the **Contents** field with the following values:
    - **Target**: `Magento Global Configuration (./app/etc)`
    - **Path**: `/modules/Foggyline_Stripe.xml`
    - **Type**: `File`
    - **Include**: `-leave blank-`
    - **Ignore**: `-leave blank-`, or possibly add a file to ignore, such as `.git` or `.DS_Store`, something you would not like to package

    Now, click on the **Add Contents Path** button again; this will add the second row of data that you need to fill with the following values:

    - **Target**: `Magento Community module file (./app/code/community)`
    - **Path**: `/Foggyline/Stripe`
    - **Type**: `Recursive Dir`
    - **Include**: `-leave blank-`
    - **Ignore**: `-leave blank-`, or possibly add a file to ignore, such as `.git` or `.DS_Store`, something you would not like to package

9. Remain on the **Contents** section, without going to the **Load Local Package** section, and click on the **Save Data and Create Package** button. This saves the form data in a package data file and creates an extension package file.

The package data file is an XML document that stores the rules for building the package. This file is saved on the disk in the `MAGENTO/var/connect/` folder. Based on the data we filled in previously, this would generate a `MAGENTO/var/connect/Foggyline_Stripe.xml` file.

The Extension Package file contains all source code needed. This file is saved on the disk in the `MAGENTO/var/connect/` folder, more precisely `MAGENTO/var/connect/Foggyline_Stripe-1.0.0.tgz`. You should try to unpack the `Foggyline_Stripe-1.0.0.tgz` file to confirm that the structure of its files and folders is correct. In addition, the archive includes another file created by the packager `package.xml`, more precisely `MAGENTO/var/connect/package.xml`. It contains information about the extension, such as the description of the structure of files and folders included in the package, and the md5 sum for each file. Overall, this file is the description of the extension containing instructions about how to install it by listing paths to files and target locations to place them. It also includes validation that the extension is correctly formed and that the contents still match with what was created.

This concludes the process of creating an extension package. Now that our extension package file is ready, it can be uploaded to Magento Connect.

Creating an extension profile

The extension profile page describes your extension. Magento Connect forces specific design guides for extensions, which you must follow or risk the extension not being approved. You can obtain the design guideline from `http://www.magentocommerce.com/magento-connect/create_your_extension`.

Besides design guidelines, a good extension profile should also include other important information that users may need to be aware of to configure the extension, as well as contact information for support questions.

To create an extension profile, perform the following steps:

1. Log in to `http://www.magentocommerce.com`.
2. From the top-right of the page, click on **My Account**, and then click on your avatar image or username to access your account dashboard.
3. From the left-side bar, click on **Developers** to expand its options.
4. From the expanded **Developers** panel, click on **Add New Extension**. In case you get a **Terms and Conditions** screen presented at this point, click on the **Agree** button to proceed. You should now see a screen similar to the following screenshot partially shown:

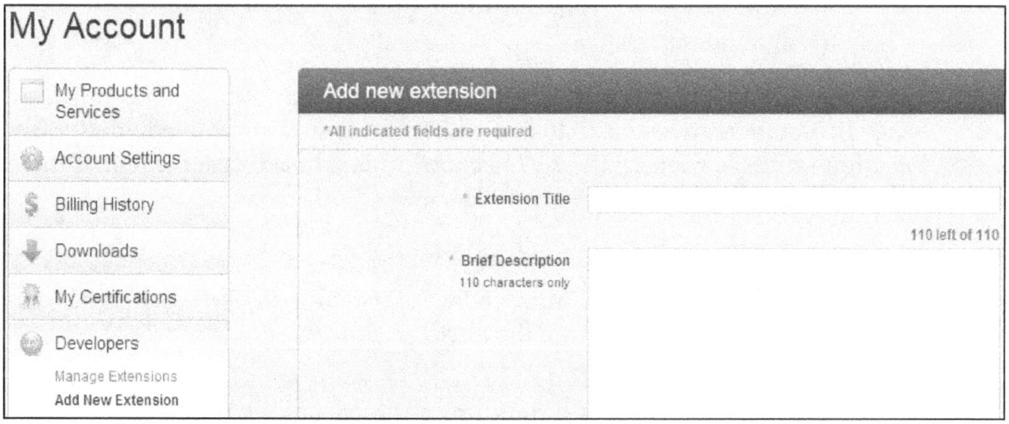

5. Now, start filling in the following form fields:
   - **Extension Title** is a required field. There should be a short descriptive title that explains your extension. Put something, such as `Stripe by Foggyline`.
   - **Brief Description** is a required field. Use this value to briefly describe the extension's functionality, in a clear text format. You could put something, such as `Stripe payment implementation` here.

- **Detailed Description** is a required field. Use it to describe the extension's functionality in depth, or at least in enough detail for a user to understand its purpose. This field supports certain HTML elements. Just for the sake of simplicity, you could put something as `Stripe payment implementation extension` here.
- **Extension Key** is a required field. The value provided here must be the exact same name you used during the packaging process under **Package Info | Name**. It is case-sensitive.
- **Extension Categories** is a required field. It allows you to set one or more categories, or subcategories of this extension, with its functionality. Categories and subcategories classify your extension so that merchants can more easily find it in Magento Connect. Select **Show/Hide** subcategories to expand the subcategory menu, then select the **Checkout**, **Payment**, and **Gateways** options.
- **Extension Locale** is a required field. Here, you select the languages supported in the extension package. Since we haven't worked with Magento translation functionality so far, we can select **English (United States) / English (United States)** as a locale.
- **Extension Icon** is a required field for both the label and the image upload. The image that you provide here will be your extension's default image and it should adhere to the Magento Connect design guidelines.

Next, we come to the Community fieldset that has a number of input fields as well. However, it seems that all of the form fields are disabled. Under the **Versions** section, click on the **1.7** checkbox; this will activate the rest of the form fields that you should fill as follows:

- **Is Free** is an optional field. Select it.
- **License Type** is a required field. Set its value to **OSL**, as it needs to match the value from the package process.
- **License Name** is a read-only field. Its value should now read **Open Software License**, as it did during the packaging process.
- **License URL** is a read-only field. Its value is a link labeled as **Official license website**.
- **Versions** is a multiple checkbox field starting from 1.0 all the way to 1.7. Select **version 1.7** only.

6. Click on the **Save** button to create this extension profile. If saved properly, you will be redirected to your extensions list under **My Extensions** as shown in the following screenshot:

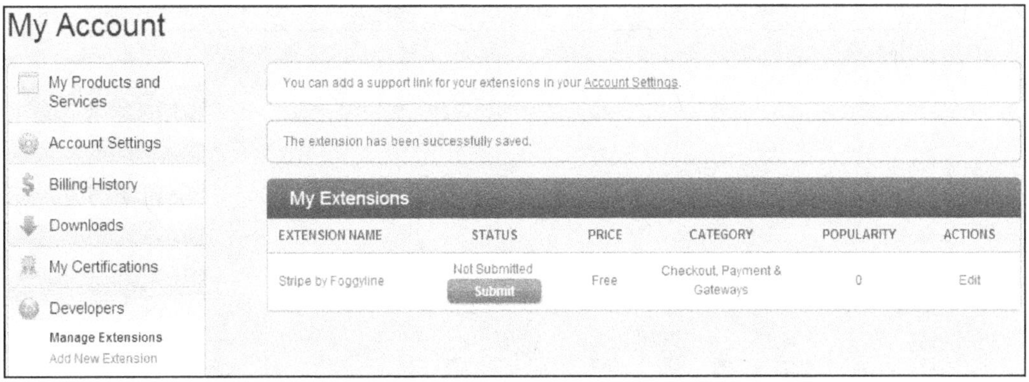

Uploading the extension package

Even though we were able to save the extension profile page, there is one more important piece of the puzzle missing, the extension package itself. Strangely, Magento Connect does not allow us to upload the extension package from the same screen where we define the overall information of our extension as we just did. In order to upload the actual extension package, perform the following steps:

1. Make sure that you are still on the **My Extensions** page, which is actually **My Account** | **Developer** | **Manage Extensions page**.
2. Click on the **Edit** link next to your **Stripe** by `Foggyline` extension. This should open almost the same screen, as we did while creating an extension profile steps. The main difference with this screen is that we have two new tabs at the top, **Screenshots** and **Versions**.

If you open up the Screenshots tab, there should already be a single screenshot, which you uploaded during the steps performed in the *Creating an extension profile* section. Even though it's a good practice to add several screenshots of your extension functionality, we will focus our attention on the Versions tab, because this is where we actually upload the extension package.

To upload the extension package, perform the following steps:

1. Click on the **Versions** tab. You should see a screen similar to the following screenshot:

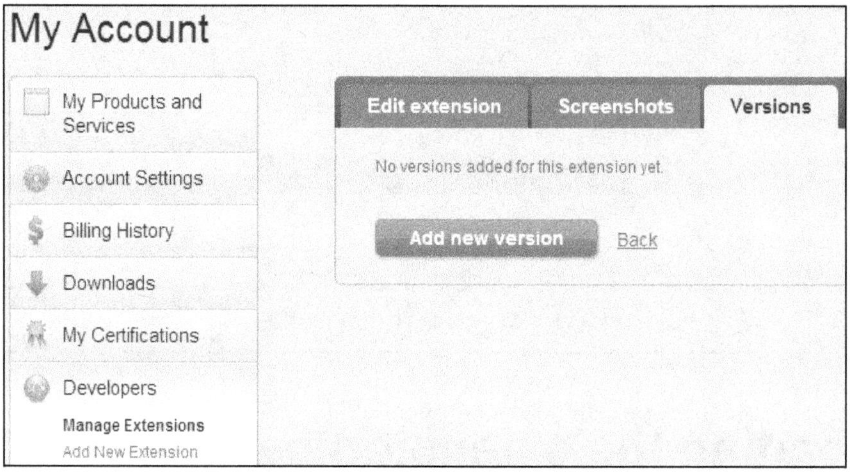

2. Click on the **Add new version** button. This should take you to a new page, as shown on the following screenshot:

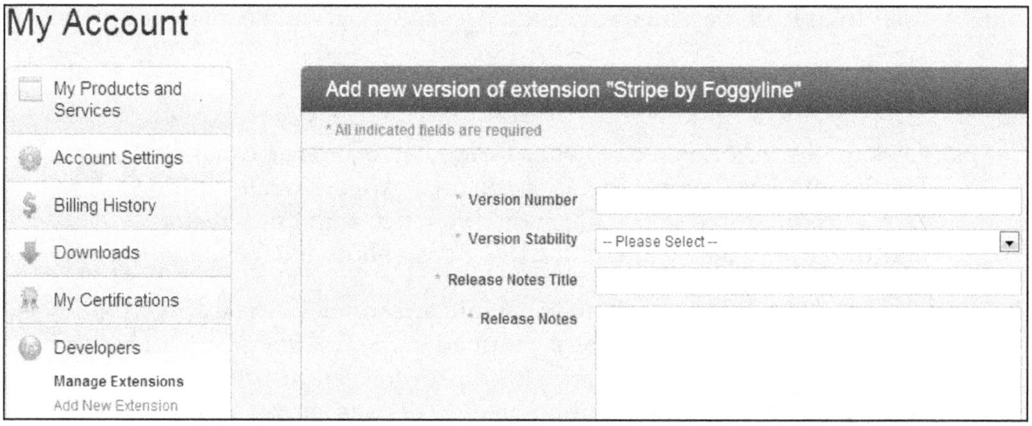

3. Fill in all required fields with the same information used during the extension packaging process, then click on the **Continue to upload** button. This should take you to a screen, as shown in the following screenshot:

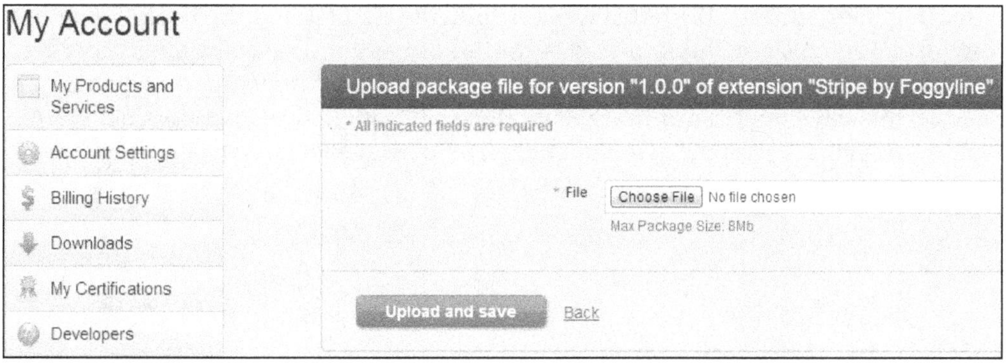

4. Finally, choose a `MAGENTO/var/connect/Foggyline_Stripe-1.0.0.tgz` file to upload, and click on the **Upload and save** button. If all went well, you would see a screen with the success message **Package has been successfully uploaded to Magento Connect channel ver.2.0**, as shown in the following screenshot:

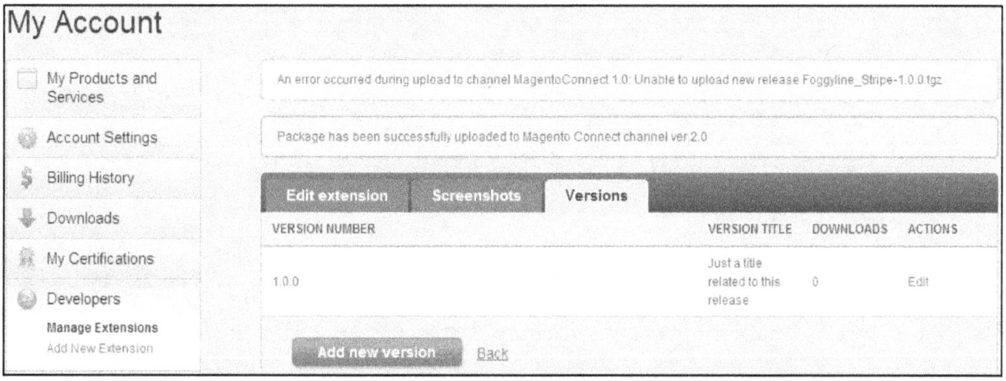

You may also see the error message **An error occurred during upload to channel MagentoConnect 1.0: Unable to upload new release Foggyline_Stripe-1.0.0.tgz**. However, this is not an error you should be concerned with. Our extension was built for Magento 1.7 and newer, where Magento Connect Channel 2.0 is used for packaging. The error you see here is just the Magento upload system telling you that it did not get the package for Magento Connect Channel 1.0, which is fine.

Summary

In this chapter, we learned how to package and distribute our custom extensions. This knowledge will most certainly be of use if you plan on selling your extensions, or sharing them for free. With this we conclude the chapter and the book. Hopefully, you got enough insight and knowledge for building your own extensions. There are a lot of caveats that you might find along the way. Just remember, Magento has a very active developer community over at `http://www.magentocommerce.com/boards` and `http://magento.stackexchange.com/`, so feel free to ask for help.

Index

Symbols

A

B

C

D

E

F

G

H

I

S

T

U

V

X

Z

[PACKT] open source
community experience distilled
PUBLISHING

Mastering Magento

ISBN: 978-1-849516-94-5 Paperback: 300 pages

Maximize the power of Magento: for developers, designers, and store owners

1. Learn how to customize your Magento store for maximum performance
2. Exploit little-known techniques for extending and tuning your Magento installation.
3. Step-by-step guides for making your store run faster, better, and more productively

---

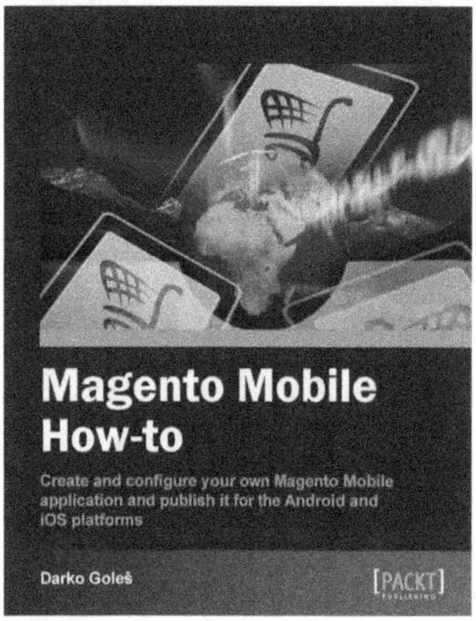

Magento Mobile How-to

ISBN: 978-1-849693-66-0 Paperback: 78 pages

Create and configure your own Magento Mobile application and publish it for the Android and iOS platforms

1. Learn something new in an Instant! A short, fast, focused guide delivering immediate results
2. Style and theme your Magento Mobile Application interface
3. Configure Product categories and add static content for mobile
4. Prepare and publish your Magento mobile application targeting iPhone/iPad and Android platforms

Please check **www.PacktPub.com** for information on our titles

[PACKT] open source
community experience distilled
PUBLISHING

Magento Beginner's Guide - Second Edition

ISBN: 978-1-782162-70-4 Paperback: 320 pages

Learn how to create a fully featured, attractive online store with the most powerful open source solution for e-commerce

1. Install, configure, and manage your own e-commerce store
2. Extend and customize your store to reflect your brand and personality
3. Handle tax, shipping, and custom orders

Magento 1.3 Sales Tactics Cookbook

ISBN: 978-1-849510-12-7 Paperback: 292 pages

Improve your Magento store's sales and increase your profits with this collection of simple and effective tactical techniques

1. Build a professional Magento sales website, with the help of easy-to-follow steps and ample screenshots, to solve real-world business needs and requirements
2. Develop your website by using your creativity and exploiting the sales techniques that suit your needs
3. Provide visitors with attractive and innovative features to make your site sell

Please check **www.PacktPub.com** for information on our titles

www.ingramcontent.com/pod-product-compliance
Lightning Source LLC
LaVergne TN
LVHW081346050326
832903LV00024B/1345
* 9 7 8 1 7 8 3 2 8 0 3 9 1 *